Leadership for Quality

SERIES EDITOR
BARRIE DALE
UMIST

Leadership for Quality

STRATEGIES FOR ACTION

Frances Clark

McGRAW-HILL BOOK COMPANY
London · New York · St Louis · San Francisco · Auckland
Bogotá · Caracas · Lisbon · Madrid · Mexico · Milan
Montreal · New Delhi · Panama · Paris · San Juan
São Paulo · Singapore · Sydney · Tokyo · Toronto

Published by
McGRAW-HILL Book Company Europe
Shoppenhangers Road, Maidenhead, Berkshire SL6 2QL, England
Telephone: 01628 23432
Fax: 01628 770224

British Library Cataloguing in Publication Data
Clark, Frances A.
  Leadership for Quality: Strategies for
  Action. – (Quality in Action Series)
  I. Title   II. Series
  658.562

  ISBN 0-07-707828-4

Library of Congress Cataloging-in-Publication Data
Clark, Frances A.
    Leadership for quality: strategies for action/Frances Clark.
      p.   cm.
    ISBN 0-07-707828-4 (pbk. : alk. paper)
    1. Total quality management.   I. Title.
  HD62.15.C538
  658.5'62–dc20   95-37231
                                                                  CIP

Copyright © 1996 McGraw-Hill International (UK) Limited. All rights reserved.
No part of this publication may be reproduced, stored in a retrieval system, or
transmitted, in any form or by any means, electronic, mechanical, photocopying,
recording, or otherwise, without the prior permission of McGraw-Hill International
(UK) Limited.

12345 BL 99876

Typeset by BookEns Ltd., Royston, Herts.
Printed and bound in Great Britain by Biddles Ltd., Guildford, Surrey.

Printed on permanent paper in compliance with ISO Standard 9706.

Contents

Series Preface

Quality is regarded by most producers, customers and consumers as more important than ever before in their manufacturing, service and purchasing strategies. If you doubt this just think of the unsatisfactory examples of quality you have personally experienced, the bad feelings it gave you, the resulting actions you took and the people you told about the experience and the outcomes. The concept of Total Quality Management (TQM) is increasingly being adopted by organizations as the means of satisfying the needs and expectations of their customers.

Total quality management has been practised by the major Japanese manufacturing companies for the last 30 or so years. Their commitment to continuous and company-wide quality improvement has provided them with the foundation by which they have been able to capture markets the world over. In response to this competitive pressure Western manufacturing companies, first in America and then Europe, started to embrace the TQM ethic; this was followed by commercial and service-type organizations. The superior performing Western organizations have now some 15 or so years of operating experience of TQM. These organizations have now integrated the principles and practices of TQM into the way they run their business. This is one indicator of the effectiveness of TQM. Senior management are judged on results, and if TQM does not improve business performance they would simply rechannel the resources in other directions.

Total quality management is a subject and management philosophy in which there appears to be an unquenchable thirst for knowledge, despite the considerable volume of published material. In recent times the interest in TQM has been fuelled by the Malcolm Baldridge National Quality Award and the European Quality Award. These awards, based on a model of TQM, are increasingly being used by organizations as part of their business improvement process. This interest in the subject has continued in spite of some surveys and reports indicating that TQM is not working. There is also evidence that the concept is being regurgitated under a number of other guises. The objective of this major 'Quality in Action' book series is to help satisfy this need and fill what we believe are gaps in the existing range of current books. It is also obvious from the arguments advanced from some quarters that there is still a lack of understanding of TQM and what it is about. Hopefully the books in the series will help to improve the level of understanding.

McGraw-Hill has already published books by three of the best known and internationally respected quality management experts – Crosby, Feigenbaum and Juran. The 'Quality in Action' series will build upon the work of these three men; this in itself will be a challenge.

I was honoured when asked by McGraw-Hill to be the 'Quality in Action' book series editor. I have personally been involved in industrially based TQM research for the last 14 or so years and from this experience believe I am well placed to identify the aspects of TQM which need to be addressed by new books on the subject.

The prime focus of the series is management and the texts have been prepared from this standpoint. However, undergraduate and postgraduate students will also find the books of considerable benefit in understanding the concept, principles, elements and practices of TQM, the associated quality management systems, tools and techniques, the means of introducing, developing and sustaining TQM and the associated difficulties, and how to integrate TQM into the business practices of an organization.

One objective of the series is to provide some general TQM reading as guidance for management in introducing, developing and sustaining a process of continuous and company-wide quality improvement. It will focus on manufacturing, commercial and service situations. We are looking for recognized writers (academics, consultants and practitioners) who will be able to address the subject from a European perspective. The books appearing on this theme will not duplicate already published material; rather they will build upon, enhance and develop the TQM wisdom and address the subject from a new perspective. A second objective is to provide texts on aspects of TQM not adequately covered by current books (for example, TQM and human resources, sustaining TQM, TQM: corporate culture and organizational change, partnership sourcing and supply chain management, TQM and business strategy. It is likely that the authors of these books will be from disciplines (e.g. accounting, economic, psychology, human resources) not traditionally associated with quality management. A third objective is to provide texts which deal with quality management systems, tools and techniques in a practical 'how-to' manner.

The first four books in the series, dealing with understanding Japanese-led companies to make them your customers, making quality of service really work, achieving business success through reward and recognition, and communicating change, have been well received by the business community and are helping to address these objectives.

My commitment to this series is that I am prepared to allocate time from my considerable research, teaching and advisory activities in order to ensure that it meets and hopefully exceeds the needs and expectations of our readers.

B.G. Dale, Series Editor

About the Series Editor

Dr Barrie Dale is Reader in Quality Management at the Manchester School of Management, UMIST and Director of the UMIST Quality Management Centre. The Centre is involved in three major activities: research into Total Quality Management; the Centre houses the Ford Motor Company Northern Regional Centre for training suppliers in Statistical Process Control; and the operation of a Total Quality Management Multi-Company Teaching Programme involving collaborators from a variety of industrial and business environments. He also coordinates the Bowater Corrugated Division Multi-Institute Teaching Programme. Dr Dale is also a Non-Executive Director of Manchester Circuits Ltd, a company specializing in the manufacture of high technology and complex printed circuit boards.

He is co-editor of the *International Journal of Quality and Reliability Management,* now in its twelfth volume. Dr Dale is co-author of *Managing Quality, Quality Costing, Quality Improvement Through Standards, Total Quality and Human Resources: An Executive Guide* and *The Road to Quality* and has published more than 220 papers on the subject of quality management. Dr Dale has also led four missions to Japan of European executives to study the application of TQM in major Japanese manufacturing organizations. He is the international quality management adviser to the South African Quality Institute and has also been closely associated with the Hong Kong Government Industry Department in preparing a series of booklets on quality management for their 'Make it Better in Hong Kong' campaign.

Preface

Questioned by one of my children (then six years old) as to why I was working at home that Friday, I replied: 'To write a book on leadership for quality.' 'What does that mean?' he persisted. 'It's like this. What would your headmaster need to do to make your school even better?' 'Care about it even more,' came the instant reply.

A simple answer to a complex question. So I repeated the enquiry with his ten-year-old sister, who was equally swift: 'See that the pupils are looked after and find out from them what needs improving.'

Intrigued by the ability of children to pinpoint the heart of the matter very quickly, I tried it on my third child. In contrast with the others, there was a long and anxious pause: 'Oh, that's not fair! That's much too difficult for me to answer,' was the angry reply.

These responses capture, in an uncomplicated way, some of the key dilemmas of leading a quality programme: not being satisfied with the status quo and wanting to change it; believing wholeheartedly in the concept and caring about the outcome; and recognizing that the journey will not be easy.

For all the flagship organizations and their acclaimed successes there are also many unreported failures. The rationale for this book is that, while it has become fashionable to criticize quality programmes for non-delivery of results, a key differentiating theme in all this is leadership. The history of many of the long-standing organizations which are pioneers in the field of quality in the UK, USA and Japan shows the importance of their founders in generating a quality-led approach to business through being a role model in the treatment of their customers. Mr Sieff of Marks and Spencer, Mr Hewlett of Hewlett Packard and Mr Honda of Honda are some classic examples.

Yet to talk of leadership as if it only existed at the very top of the organization misses the point, and to assume a cultural similarity of leadership with such a range of examples oversimplifies the situation. Leadership and management will be exercised at much lower levels within the organization and in a way which will suit both national and corporate cultures.

This book does not attempt to profile the traits and competences of effective leaders at the top of successful companies, as this approach has a long history of searching in vain for the 'Holy Grail'. Furthermore, competences in one organization may appear as weaknesses in another, depending on the culture. Instead, it outlines what leaders and managers, regardless of function, can do to create and sustain their quality drives, providing examples from successful organizations. It is intended for those managers who may not think of themselves as quality specialists but who want to make a contribution. This may take the form of being a sponsor, adviser, implementor, assessor or line manager affected by a programme. It should also make them confident in choosing and applying some of the frameworks and tools in their own areas, using external assistance if necessary, and in overcoming the concerns and challenges they will meet along the way.

Acknowledgements

The first acknowledgement must be to the managers on executive programmes who created the demand for an input on quality and the course directors who encouraged me to fulfil it. The Doctoral and MBA students were unrelentless in their interest in the subject, with their quality dilemmas, and endless theses and dissertations for supervision. I thank my colleagues in the Quality Group at Henley Management College for their support and encouragement, especially in the early stages. Fellow consultants at Philips Electronics and Coopers and Lybrand worked with me on customer-oriented and quality-related projects and passed on much knowledge. The European Foundation for Quality Management has helped to increase my understanding. Organizations such as Royal Mail enabled me to conduct research and provided a useful sounding board. For this I am very grateful.

Finally, my family has enhanced the quality of my working life by always being around to offer their support and, in some cases, a much needed distraction. To Nicola, Antony and Christopher, my husband Roger and father Alex, I give my undivided attention from now on (until the next time!)

Leadership in action: an overview

1.1 INTRODUCTION

Pick up a book on quality management, ask the quality gurus what makes for success or search for some comfort among the debris of a wrecked programme and somewhere will be a statement about the need for 'commitment from top management'.

Quite so! But how do you recognize commitment beyond the obvious examples of courting the media, signing off resources and 'wandering around?' What exactly are organizational leaders supposed to *do*? The folklore of quality success suggests that, apart from possessing the inevitable charisma, 40 or so competences and boundless energy and enthusiasm, leaders must sustain people's commitment indefinitely. The more realistic view shows that success lies more within their recognition that the management of quality relies on the harnessing of several different functional perspectives and practices:

- *strategy* (linking the business direction to its actual and potential customers);
- *marketing* (understanding the customer's needs);
- *human resource and organization transformation* (motivating and supporting people to meet those needs with a suitable structure and culture);
- *operations management* (the management of systems and processes to deliver them).

The skilful leader for quality, then, is not the superperson of quality mythology but an analyst, integrator and facilitator of the impact of these different areas in his or her own appropriate niche in the organization.

This book takes a critical look at the practical issues leaders confront when involved with quality and, as such, presents a synthesis of these underlying themes. Each chapter ends with some 'action questions' to see how the issues raised are being tackled in readers' own organizations. This first chapter provides an introduction to definitions of quality, some frameworks for examining leadership while also addressing the issue of whether leaders are different from managers. These two words will be used interchangeably, since the debate in the literature continues. In practice, the distinction is one of emphasis: managers may be required to lead, and leaders may have to manage, depending on the circumstances. Furthermore, some would say that the question is a non-starter, as leadership lives in a relationship, not in an organizational position. The chapter concludes with a brief look at leadership in other countries and an analysis of what can happen when leadership for quality fails. A framework of the broad areas leaders need to consider when involved with quality is then presented, which also serves as the structure for the rest of the book.

1.2 DEFINITIONS OF QUALITY AND THE MANAGER'S ROLE

It is not the intention to undertake here a review of the ideas of the major gurus on quality, but to highlight the role of leadership and management. However, it is worth pausing to reflect on the various definitions of quality, as their adoption can affect the way in which quality is introduced and led within the organization, as well as influencing the commitment of its employees. Not only does the definition of quality differ according to the guru consulted, but its meaning varies with the individual customer. Quality can therefore be an illusive concept if taken out of context.

One view[1] is that quality is the 'meeting of customers' needs' (not designing a product and then attempting to sell it) and ensuring that it does so in a uniform way. Any variation should be predictable, or at least controllable and that 95 per cent of the time; problems have their origins in the processes within an organization rather than with individuals. Management's responsibility in this situation is to ensure that the system for producing a quality product is stable and capable of performing to requirements. It should also produce a culture in which employees feel comfortable and are respected, to ensure that a quality output is delivered.

Leaders should therefore help people to do a better job, not tamper with the system, since that only increases variation. It is their responsibility to remove poor systems and to support their staff rather than be expected to directly motivate them. Commitment will follow if people feel they have the means and right environment to do a good job.

Another view[2] is that quality means 'fitness for use'. Attention to the customer's needs in the design process is crucial, and error-free work is the way of ensuring customer satisfaction. While the customer's requirements are key, a product's quality can only be truly assessed when it is actually in use. To implement a programme of quality successfully, three stages are necessary: quality planning, quality control and quality improvement. The first stage sets out the philosophy and goals, the second carefully monitors work as it is carried out, and the third involves commitment and resources. The role of management is to lead by action, not just engage in direction-setting for their staff, as the majority of problems related to quality can be laid at management's door.

'Conformance to requirements'[3] is another often quoted definition, but it does not indicate whose requirements (customers?, technical specialists?, marketing? or management?). If this is left undefined in, say, a technologically driven company, the kind of comment often to be heard is: 'Why do we make a Rolls-Royce when a Mini will do?' Products are over-engineered and rarely show the kind of profit margins that such an investment should bring. The standard of performance for quality products or services with this definition is 'zero defects', ruling out a slightly imperfect output which might be acceptable to the customer if it falls within agreed limits. However, the very idea of acceptable levels of quality implies that it is legitimate to make errors, which is contrary to the whole approach. Quality here is measured by the costs of non-conformance. In this scheme, management are said to be responsible for 85 per cent of the errors, and so their mission is to reduce this by raising the awareness of the need for quality, leading by example, and providing resources to meet quality targets. They should also encourage cross-functional teams to solve problems, which itself increases understanding.

A fourth approach [4] is also based on the notion of 'conformance to requirements', but should be driven by a strong market focus, underpinned by a sound understanding of the competition, emphasizing customer needs. Management should attach a high degree of importance to being close to the customer in order to find out his or her requirements and lead by example. Here it is management's role to see that prevention of poor quality is the goal that everyone strives to attain. Therefore management should be proactive, first asking: 'Are we capable of doing the job correctly?', not 'Have we done the job correctly?' The indispensable factor in ensuring that the quality system works is management commitment.

An alternative framework[5] focuses not only on a customer orientation but on the 'life cycle' of a product and the involvement of all the departments in its production. Quality is:

> the total composite production and service characteristics of marketing, engineering, manufacturing and maintenance through which the product or service in use will meet the customer's expectations.

Quality does not mean 'outright excellence', but the 'best for satisfying certain customer conditions'. These are often called the characteristics of the good or service (reliability, serviceability and so on). Meeting these should become a key part of business strategy for which accountabilities are clear:

> ... implementation of customer-orientated quality activities is a prime responsibility of general management and of the main line operations of marketing, engineering, production, industrial relations, finance and service as well as of the quality control function itself.

With this approach, every manager – functional, line or staff – has to be involved in the quality approach. As the product or service moves through the life cycle, the customer's definition of quality may change and management must be alert to this.

The focus on quality as part of business strategy has also been emphasized[6] and this will be elaborated in Chapter 2. It puts the onus on management to pick only those aspects of quality (from a potentially large number) that the customer values and to deliver only those in order to compete successfully. Management's role is to monitor continuously which of those dimensions is the key to customer satisfaction and ensure that the organization excels in them.

However, merely meeting customers' requirements may not be enough.[7] Expectations rise continuously, and to differentiate one's offering one must 'delight the customer' by exceeding his or her expectations. 'Fitness for use' is the minimum criterion. In time, today's extra features become tomorrow's standard, so perceived quality is continuously driven up. Management's role here is to avoid the complacency which follows the reputation for success, and to monitor the environment and its potential impact on the capability to deliver the necessary quality.

Public sector services are also engaged in the search for quality, and they often have to satisfy the needs of several customers, perhaps with conflicting demands, who may be temporary or permanent, and with different values or power bases.[8] For example, there are three types (definitions) of quality in the UK health service[9]:

- client quality (for patients and carers)
- professional quality (for providers and referrers)
- management quality (for those who run the service)

and for those groups which are in the health service quality may be defined as:

> fully meeting the needs of those who need the service most, at the lowest cost to the organization, within limits and directives set by higher authorities and purchasers.

This definition allows for the fact that it may not always be advisable to define quality in terms of client satisfaction and stated demands. For example, a patient may not always know what he or she needs, or may ask for some treatment which is potentially harmful. Another definition of quality [10] stresses the importance of the customer's expectations:

> how consistently the product or service delivered meets or exceeds the customer's (internal or external) expectations and needs.

The management behaviour required for total quality is therefore:

> the management of all the resources, systems and procedures to ensure this happens, including the relationship with suppliers and distributors.

This definition also stresses the need to ensure that a sound infrastructure is in place to support any quality programme – a factor which is often overlooked and can lead to failure.

Another attempt to define quality as it applied to business identified five perspectives:[11]

1 *Transcendental* (quality is a 'universal' and 'absolute' equivalent to uncompromising high standards on the functional requirements of a specific product. Quality is established by experience.)

2 *Product-oriented* (quality is precise and measurable and reflected in quantifiable product attributes).

3 *User-oriented* (quality is in the perception of the user and not in the product *per se*).

4 *Process-oriented* (quality is adhering to prescribed specifications and getting it right first time).

5 *Value-based* (a quality product is one which meets a specific need at a price which is acceptable).

The view taken was that marketing and sales would usually subscribe to the third definition, production to the fourth and R&D to the second. The first and last views might be those taken by other functions. This diversity may cause problems: if an organization does not integrate these kinds of differences, its competitive position may be damaged if there is no internal agreement as to what constitutes quality for that organization. This problem of defining quality will be dealt with in the next chapter, since it has implications for strategy and the resources committed to its delivery.

In summary, then, whatever definition of quality is chosen, some key themes emerge for the role of leadership: customer orientation, commitment, measurement, control, continuous improvement, and motivation. What they have in common is that quality is part of a business strategy running through the entire organization (see Chapter 2). While all these definitions exist, any product or service quality is judged by the interests of different stakeholders (shareholders, customers, staff and the community). These may be enshrined in the various mission and value statements of the organization. Their relative order and emphasis give a clue as to how that organization will be led towards achieving its goal of quality. However, while they embody the broad outlines of what the organization should do, leaders play a role in their interpretation.

1.3 WHY HAVE LEADERS?

Traditionally, leaders, at whatever organizational level, exist to help make sense of the world for their followers. They extract order out of chaos and manage and protect the boundaries of their work group to allow their staff to do their jobs without being buffeted by organizational storms. In the field of quality, the leader is needed more than ever at every level because quality is not only a way of thinking but a discipline which has developed out of necessity and practice. It has yielded frameworks and techniques and a growing body of knowledge which has had its failures as well as its successes. It has pointed up best practice, rather than had a coherent set of theoretical underpinnings which are then applied in a systematic way. Its strength (and potential weakness) is that it is related to every major discipline, yet cannot be successful by following the approaches of only one.

Among all this diversity, leaders, then, have to pick their way carefully: decide which definitions of quality they will choose in relation to their organization's strategic needs and which set of values they will espouse. They will need to be aware of, and perhaps even resist, some of the less helpful pressures to pursue the quality route:

- 'me too' programmes because of the competition
- cost reduction under another name
- demand from customers to be accredited quickly for various standards or awards.

Sound judgement will also be necessary, since there are numerous approaches to delivering quality and as many consultants willing to become indispensable in its pursuit.

Once the change process is underway, a climate has to be set and maintained so that quality can take hold. For example, standards need to be set, new working practices created, problem identification encouraged and changes in management style developed. The leader has to ensure that all these requirements dovetail and support each other and that resources are available to ensure consistency of the quality message.

After the programme has been put in place, leaders are needed to refocus and redouble the effort. The original enthusiasm may have waned, and new campaigns are necessary. Many drives with a quality component started in the 1980s (Fig. 1.1) are now being renamed or refocused in order to create enthusiasm. Some organizations have had several, but only a few are listed here.

All this is not merely cosmetic. A continuous improvement philosophy demands an upgrading of services in line with customers' expectations. The

Organization	Programme	Other initiative
British Airways	Customer First	Winning for Customers
British Telecom	Project Sovereign	Breakout
Royal Mail	Customer First	Business Excellence

FIGURE 1.1   Quality-related drives

leader has to anticipate this and take appropriate action to bring this about at the relevant level in the organization.

Leaders are also vital in managing expectations inside and outside the organization. Various stakeholders may have unrealistic or inaccurate ideas about the possible range or impact of benefits of a quality approach and the timing of their delivery. This is important, as finance, credit or other resources could be withheld or withdrawn permanently if promises do not appear to have been kept.

1.4 CHARISMATIC LEADERS: DO THEY EXIST?

The idea of a charismatic business leader is today taking a battering from the management gurus. One position[12] is that charismatic leaders are not necessarily good for the organization and that, in any case, effective leadership does not depend on charisma: 'Indeed, charisma becomes the undoing of leaders. It makes them inflexible, convinced of their own infallibility, and unable to change'.

After an analysis of great leaders comes the conclusion that, since no two personalities studied had similar qualities, the notion of common traits as an explanation for this charisma does not help us understand the phenomenon any better. The view expressed is that leadership is, above all else, work involving an analysis of the organization's mission: 'defining it and establishing it clearly and visibly ... to be the trumpet that sounds a clear sound'.

Similarly, the work of researchers[13] has done much to dispel some of the myths surrounding leadership which can discourage possible leaders from taking on this role:
- leadership is a rare skill
- leaders are born, not made

- leaders are charismatic
- leadership exists at the top of an organization
- the leader controls, directs, manipulates.

Taking each in turn, it can be said first that, although there is a scarcity of great leaders, there is some potential for leadership in all of us. The army recognizes this with the saying that 'in every private's rucksack is a field marshall's baton'. Moreover, leadership is not something which is practised all the time. Individuals can be leaders on one occasion and followers on another.

Secondly, leaders are not necessarily born. Many may have had a difficult childhood or problems to overcome before they had the confidence to lead others. There is also ample anecdotal and evidential support to conclude that leadership can be learned (as the number of courses on this topic for managers testifies) and always improved.

Thirdly, as for leaders being charismatic, some may indeed have this elusive quality. However, the view is that where charisma does exist it is probably something that flows from being effective rather than being its cause. Effective leaders such as Henderson of ICI, or Weinstock of GEC are not particularly charismatic, yet have led their organizations successfully.

Fourthly, it is precisely because of the publicity surrounding some Chief Executive Officers (CEOs) that people come to associate leadership with behaviour and attitudes at the top of the organization only. The reality is that whenever a small group comes together to achieve something, a leader (not necessarily a formal one) is needed for the group to be most effective and this role may rotate.

Finally, the view of the leader as a controller and manipulator is counter-productive, since leadership can achieve more by empowering others and offering them a goal towards which they can direct their energies. In fact, the complete opposite of these various myths is the cornerstone on which the quality movement and its programmes are built.

1.5 TRANSACTIONAL OR TRANSFORMATIONAL LEADERSHIP?

Attempting to move and coordinate the efforts of others can happen in several ways. Some will be concerned primarily with the 'transactions' to keep the organization on course and maintain the status quo; others will aim to 'transform' it. Various writers on organizations and management have made the distinction, which approximates to management and leadership respectively. One view[14] which sums this up is that:

> Most US corporations are overmanaged and underled .... The real challenge is
> to combine strong leadership and strong management and use each to balance
> the other.

The contrasting patterns of behaviours and views of each are summarized in Fig. 1.2. However, this does not mean that individuals cannot do both; possession of skills in one area does not necessarily preclude skills in another.

Leaders	*Managers*
● coping with change	● coping with complexity
● setting direction	● planning and budgeting
● aligning people	● organization and staffing
● motivating and inspiring	● controlling and problem solving

FIGURE 1.2   What leaders do

Coping with change requires leaders to be alert to the interplay of environmental factors which shape and constrain the capabilities of the organization. They must decide when and how to adapt to change in order to survive. In contrast, management are not unaware of this, but the prime task is to unravel and work through the complexities of organizational life, generating standards and some consistency in the way in which work is done.

Setting the direction of an organization involves absorbing a vast amount of disparate and even conflicting information. This has to be synthesized into a view or vision of the future which is based as much on intuition as on analysis and on the willingness to take calculated risks. How this can be achieved is left to the managers themselves. In order to manage this uncertainty and complexity it is necessary to plan and budget, even though managers know there may be some variation. Without this process, managers cannot begin to set targets and evolve the means for achieving them through the judicious allocation of resources.

When organizations need to change, groups and individuals have to move forward together in the same direction. Aligning hearts and minds is the challenge presented to leaders. The message has to be communicated in a way which is credible and which can be reinterpreted in relation to each job as the individual internalizes the vision. In the situation of change, the manager has to organize resources so that a pattern of working relationships will emerge to support the vision.

Motivating people to accept and implement change is part of the leadership role. Energy has to be released and channelled by the leader and sustained, particularly in the face of difficulties. The leaders thus emphasize the worth and value of the work people are doing, thereby enhancing the self-esteem of their staff. They involve them in decisions, coach them and acknowledge their accomplishments.

Another analysis[15] in a similar vein (Fig. 1.3) maintains that leaders are closely involved with the organization and its ideals. Therefore they are better able to derive and communicate the vision. Managers, by contrast, are said to identify more closely with the task and those doing it.

Leader	*Managers*
● involvement with institutions and ideals	● involvement with tasks and people
● commitment via inspiration	● commitment via involvement
● accountability via guilt (wants the whole person)	● accountability via contracts (wants task accomplishment)
● terminal values (end state)	● instrumental values (means to an end)
● creates problems	● fixes problems
● long-range plans	● short-term plans
● likes contrariness	● likes conformity
● intense feelings from subordinates	● flatter feelings; relations smoother, steadier

FIGURE 1.3 Leaders and managers

For leaders, work and personal life become blurred, as living for the values of the organization takes over. In contrast, the manager tries to separate the two domains in order to maintain some objectivity. Leaders gain commitment by inspiring their followers with their vision; managers are said to achieve the same end by involving their staff in what they do.

Just as the leader identifies with the organization's ideals, there is an expectation that the followers must also identify wholly with them. People are held accountable by being made to feel guilty if they are not totally involved in achieving the goals of the organization, whereas for the manager, accountability is on a more formal basis, such as job profile. The leader emphasizes long-term values which are an end in themselves; managers take a more instrumental view and see particular values as a means to an end.

As the leader seeks to transform the organization this brings change and, with it, the problems of moving from the status quo to the desired state. The leader thus creates the problems which the manager then has to fix to achieve the goals. Furthermore, plans made by the leader are long-range, in accordance with the organizational values and generate the emotional involvement of the staff. Those of the manager are shorter-term, consistent with an instrumental set of values, geared to task completion.

The ways in which each relates to his or her staff are also different. The leader with a vision does not appreciate agreement at the expense of integrity. Contrariness and a wish to challenge enables the leader to have the vision and to self-question; it also encourages followers to take risks. On the other hand, the manager who must ensure progress in the short term might find this attitude disturbing. Conformity would be a more comfortable situation in this case. Finally, the leader's implied message is: 'Love me, hate me, but don't ignore me.' The manager's feelings are not so intense or personally based, making for smoother relations with staff.

1.6 SITUATIONAL LEADERSHIP

While the leader and the manager are presented in the literature as being at opposite ends of the continuum, the reality is that these behaviours may overlap in one individual, depending on the task and the circumstances. This directs us to consider the role of situational leadership. Each leader at one level of an organization is also a follower at the next level up. A leader cannot lead if there are no staff to take the followership role. Yet what characterizes a good follower? One perspective[16] is that we are more often followers than leaders:

> So followership dominates our lives and organizations but not our thinking, because our preoccupation with leadership keeps us from considering the nature and importance of the follower.

According to this view, followers can be classified in a two-dimensional matrix of independent versus dependent critical thinking and activity versus passivity. This yields (allowing for a neutral position) a five-fold grouping of sheep; 'yes' people; alienated followers; survivors; and effective followers. These are now explained below in more detail.

The *sheep* belong to the quadrant bounded by passivity and dependent, uncritical thinking. Therefore they take no initiative; they do just as much as they are told and no more. *'Yes' people* have more life in them (being in the active and dependent quadrant), but need a leader to tell them what to do, while being deferential to suit their own ends (such as advancement in the hierarchy). The bosses they cultivate may themselves have risen in the same way, thus offering an identical role model, or be weak and need their soothing, supportive ways.

The *alienated followers* are independent, critical thinkers, but do not use these powers for the benefit of the organization. They have become cynical or do not see any benefit in offering their opinions (perhaps because they have often been rejected in the past). They therefore appear passive and uncommitted and will not overtly contradict their bosses through fear or wanting a quiet life. The *survivors* by definition, are in the middle, at the intersection of the dimensions. They offer no extremes of behaviour or attitudes and have a little of all the characteristics which will keep them safe.

Finally, there are the *effective followers*, who are critical thinkers and are prepared to act on what they believe. They are independent and go about their work energetically. They are assertive when necessary, will take calculated risks and are generally well balanced.

The quality philosophy of management depends heavily on the idea of the 'effective follower' type, possibly tolerating the 'survivors' and trying to convert them. Problem solving, empowerment and a project approach will be held back by the 'sheep', the 'yes' people and the 'alienated followers'. The effective leader has therefore to be adept in spotting and dealing with these last three groups.

The style theories of leadership are often referred to as a category in their own right. They have been included in the broader 'situational' category because they recognize the importance of certain characteristics of the follower as well as the particular task and situation which the leader has to address. Moreover, they are also related, since the outcome of a situational analysis by the leader results in the choice of a style to be used.

The Blake and Mouton grid is one such style theory.[17] It focused on two axes: concern for task and concern for people. Individuals could be high on one and low on the other and vice versa or take the middle position. This grid yielded five particular styles:

- *impoverished* (the leader is low on concern for people and the task. Therefore minimal effort is made to see that the work is done and people are not dismissed);
- *country club* (attention to relationships with people drives this leader, who sees good relationships as more important than the task. A friendly organization and a relaxed way of going about work is the key style differentiator);
- *task* (the accomplishment of the task is all-important, while relationships are secondary and operations are arranged so that the human elements cause minimal disruption);
- *middle road* (task needs and personal needs are balanced so that the work is done and morale does not suffer);
- *team* (the leader is high on meeting task needs and fulfilling relationships. Work is accomplished because of committed individuals who share a common purpose and trust.)

The approach implies that there is one best way (team style) and focuses mainly on attitudes which are then translated into behaviour rather than with the behaviours themselves. However, the team style is what quality programmes seek to attain.

Another view[18] is that two-dimensional models oversimplify the situation and that the following elements need to be examined:

- *leader style* (task-oriented or person-oriented)
- *nature of the task* (structured, detailed instructions or unstructured, new thinking required as in research or entrepreneurship)
- *the relationship between leader and follower* (liking)
- *leader's position power* (the extent to which the position itself enables the leader to offer direction).

This model too was not without criticism for its rigidity, in particular the way the leader's style was classified. However, it did highlight the emotional aspect of the relationship and the use of power. Quality programmes encourage attention to these aspects as well. They assume that employees should be happy in what they do if they are to be customer-oriented and that the power of the leader is there to be given away (empowerment) to enable them to do their job rather than comply with instructions.

Another approach introduces the idea of the team. Attention to task, team and individual needs is the focus of action-centred leadership.[19] The requirement is that to be effective, the leader's attention to the three areas should be in balance. For example, if there is an overemphasis on the team, the individual's needs may be submerged; while if there is too much time spent in satisfying individual needs, the strength and synergy of the team is reduced. If the task takes centre stage, then group morale suffers and individuals feel like a cog in the wheel, a means to an end and believe themselves to be suffering from neglect.

Situational leadership has now come to be associated with another model.[20] Like several others already described, it considers behaviour initially on two dimensions which are then modified by a third. Task (or directive behaviour) is the degree to which the leader defines the roles of the group members and directs and puts in place controls. Relationship (or supportive behaviour) is the extent to which the leader relates to group members by ensuring that communication channels are open and providing a social and emotional support. A third dimension, that of effectiveness, is basically the adaptability of the leader in selecting the appropriate style.

The behaviours associated with each position in the grid are:
- *directing* (high directive and low supportive behaviour)
- *coaching* (high directive and high supportive behaviour)
- *supporting* (high supportive and low directive behaviour)
- *delegating* (low directive and low supportive behaviour).

If, for example, the situation is ambiguous and a leader's style is directing, effective behaviour will be interpreted as having well-defined methods for accomplishing goals that are helpful to followers. In other circumstances, it will be seen as ineffective behaviour, imposing methods on others and being interested only in the short-term result.

The ability to switch effectively between the appropriate styles is called 'style flex' and is the characteristic of a mature leader. Flexibility depends on choosing an appropriate style after correctly diagnosing the situation which relates to the organization, the job itself, the leader and the follower. Each of these generates a set of expectations about appropriate behaviour; but the key ones are those of the leader and the follower. It is crucial that the leader correctly assesses the degree of competence of staff (knowledge and skills) related to the job and their commitment (determined by their motivation and confidence in themselves). These two variables together can be labelled development, and the style of leadership should ideally be matched to the varying combinations of competence and commitment.

An agreement (contract) between leader and led is necessary as to which style is appropriate for the development to occur. The idea of flexibility of style, respect for the individual and his or her development fits in well with ideas about quality implying continuous improvement of the organization, based on continuous improvement of the individual.

1.7 STRATEGIC LEADERSHIP

Strategic leadership[21] is focused more on the relationship of the leader to the organization than to an individual or group. As such, it requires leaders to perform effectively in certain strategic situations:

- start-up
- turnaround
- extracting profits from, or rationalizing, a current business
- dynamic growth in an existing business
- redeployment of efforts in an existing business
- liquidating or divesting a poorly performing business
- new acquisitions.

For example, in a turnaround situation, the organization may be suffering at the hands of the competition, leading to poor financial results. This may be compounded by inadequate systems, worsening relationships with suppliers and customers and low morale. It is therefore vital that an accurate and speedy assessment of the circumstances takes place before the leader can be effective.

According to this analysis, the strategic leader requires certain attributes to deal with a particular situation. These are skills in analysis and diagnosis (especially in the financial area), negotiation, crisis management and business strategy. The individual must also be able to handle pressure well, be energetic, a risk taker and willing to take charge. Recent examples might be Sir Ian Vallance (British Telecom) and Sir John Harvey Jones (formerly of ICI).

Skills in one situation such as turnaround may, with some additions, be useful in others. In the dynamic growth situation, a visionary perspective is necessary, as are financial planning ability and organization. The facility to pick good staff and encourage team building is also vital. It is worth noting that all the situations above which require strategic leadership, with the exception of liquidation, may be the stimulus for the initiation of a quality programme.

1.8 POWER, PURPOSE AND PROTAGONISM

Leaders have power, but this is a topic which often receives less emphasis than, say, team building, and is hardly ever considered in discussions about the implementation of quality (see Chapter 8). However, there is always an element of 'position power', which enables leaders to use their authority to make changes, even if it is in the face of some opposition. It may also give them 'reward power', so that they have the ability to impose positive and negative sanctions and allocate benefits as appropriate. In reality, the ability to provide rewards may only be the result of gaining support from superiors. 'Coercive power' (the power to withhold rewards or to obtain compliance) may also be linked with the formal position in an organization.

Over and above this, leaders may develop 'expert power', whereby competence and expertise in an area make them invaluable to their bosses or to their staff. 'Network (or lateral) power' is also an asset, as it may enable the leader to control resources or workflow informally if good alliances are formed across the organization. This may in turn depend on 'information power', acquired to suit the circumstances. Power and influence therefore mean that leaders have the ability to pursue a purpose or vision within the organization knowing that they can mobilize the necessary support from a variety of sources to make them successful protagonists of change.

1.9 LEADERSHIP IN OTHER COUNTRIES

Much of what is thought and taught in business schools about leadership has its origins in the USA and the UK and, as such, can only be part of the total picture. For example, how often is the word 'outstanding' used to describe someone who is a leader or a manager? To the Japanese this would be a misnomer because, taken literally, it would mean 'to stand outside the group'. In Japan, the leader is part of the group, sits and works in the group setting and forms an emotional bond with it. Therefore, far from being a compliment, it would imply self-seeking behaviour, placing an individual outside the group.

Any recognition of leadership by rank does not merely mean that there are privileges attached, since authority implies that the leader has responsibilities to those accepting the authority. There also has to be a consistent match between the words and the deeds of the leader. Both these aspects are very public. Japan has a culture whose sanctions are based on shame (compared with the West which is seen as a guilt culture). The breach of loyalty, trust or promises by the leader are ranked among the most serious kinds of offences, and the loss of social honour or face is the worst possible fate of executives, who will immediately resign over matters which could bring the organization into disrepute.

There are also quite striking differences between much of Western Europe and the UK in what is acceptable leader and follower behaviour. When an executive in France or Italy calls a meeting, it is essentially to pass on what has already been decided. Followers do not question the decision in a way that might be considered acceptable in the UK. To do so would be to deny the authority or expertise of the manager. With quality programmes, much of the required behaviour is exactly that: challenging, highlighting problems, and actively learning from failure, which might all be interpreted as discourteous. Empowerment may be seen as lack of competence or unwillingness to tackle change. This must raise questions about how quality programmes can be consistently implemented.

1.10 WHEN LEADERSHIP FOR QUALITY FAILS

There can be little doubt that all is not well with quality programmes (some organizations prefer not to use this term as it implies an end state), despite the well-publicized successes of Motorola, Xerox and Corning. Reports keep surfacing (within the journals dedicated to quality, more generalist ones aimed at the practising manager, and in the national and business press) that so-called quality initiatives are not delivering the anticipated results. Nevertheless, it is useful to take stock of the criticisms in an attempt to move forward by learning from past mistakes.

The evidence for this state of affairs comes from a variety of sources covering surveys, consultancies and the anecdotes of those who have been involved in these changes. In a survey of 500 US manufacturing and service companies,[22] only one-third could say that the process was 'having a significant impact'. The same source refers to a study of more than 100 firms in the UK in which respondents concluded that only 20 per cent thought their quality programmes achieved 'tangible results'.

Another survey of more than 3000 companies in the UK[23] yielded some 300 returns, 80 per cent of which were from manufacturing companies, whereas the sample had been drawn in equal proportions from manufacturing and service companies. This difference speaks for itself. The finance and insurance sectors were found to attach the lowest level of importance to quality improvement programmes. Of those companies whose programmes had run for less than three years, only 10 per cent had met their profitability targets. Of those which had been in existence for between three and seven years, 14 per cent saw no change in profit levels. Finally, some 25 per cent of companies whose programmes had lasted for between three and seven years had not reduced the cost of failure. Those initiatives which had lasted for longer than seven years had not improved customer service. Finally, a study of 40 companies[24] has made the point that many European organizations who aim to improve their quality could actually be damaging their ability to compete if they are over-zealous in attaining quality standards.

Criticisms abound that the process is extremely time-consuming, results are not visible for years, the effort required equates to that of turning an ocean-going liner and the underlying philosophy is all too vague. Some of the casualties are prestigious names such as Florida Power and Light, a gas and electricity organization which won the prestigious Deming Award for quality in 1989. Recently, it has had to reconsider the structure and organization of its programme, which had become too cumbersome in its operation.

What causes can underlie these failures? Certainly there is one theme which runs through them all at a strategic and operational level: the nature of leadership in relation to quality goals. At a strategic level, there are at least seven commonly discernible causes:

1 *Quality is not part of strategic planning and thinking* (for example, could the goal of market share be attained best by quality initiatives rather than by acquisition?)

2 *Quality is a cover for unpleasant changes* (such as cost-cutting or job loss). While BT has emphasized its progress on quality, observers may note its programme of reduction in staff numbers from 250 000 in 1988 to 170 000 in 1993, and down again to 100 000 in 1995.

3 *Quality focuses disproportionately on organizational inputs* (for example, too much information), or on conversion processes (too many procedures), or on outputs. This situation is worsened if feedback is missing, overly detailed or inappropriate.

4 *Quality lacks customer orientation* (in a technologically-driven company, professional standards may take precedence over customers' needs.

5 *Quality is adopted on a 'me-too' basis.*

6 *Over-reliance on gurus* (an 'integrated package' is sold because it is said to be tested, endorsed, thought to pose less risk and require less effort from the top of the hierarchy) .

7 *Mismanagement of expectations and time-frames*, often to satisfy short-term criteria, perhaps driven by stakeholders.

A related discussion of this problem and results-driven programmes is given in Chapter 4, 4.6, 'Avoiding the failure trap'.

Operationally, there are also many reasons for the poor performance of quality programmes:

● slavish following of guru packages, regardless of context or culture

● being driven by short-term pressures (for example, BS5750) rather than by clear objectives

● preoccupation with methodologies (statistical process control, quality circles) which only address some of the issues

● too much focus on customer care without attention to the supporting systems and structures

● over-concern with problems at the interface (assertiveness training, conflict management, interpersonal skills), which may reflect more deep-seated commercial ills)

● lack of measurables

● unempowered employees, possibly resulting in high stress and staff turnover.

All in all, they illustrate a lack of discrimination on the part of management in identifying the appropriate action to take. However, some firms have had success, so what are the differentiating factors?

One way of looking at this phenomenon[25] is the analysis of 'pioneers and followers'. A key observation is that, in the USA, the companies which have had success have been experimenting for longer than the followers. The latter were also large corporations, who, fearing being left behind, eagerly embraced the (by then) ready-packaged philosophies and techniques and then evolved their own approach. If this argument is taken further, and comparisons are made between the West and Japan,[26] then companies such as Nippondenso, Honda, Nissan, Toyota and Matsushita can each claim at least 30 or more years of experience with total quality management. For the West's leading quality exponents (Motorola, Texas Instruments, Hewlett Packard and Xerox), the figure is just over 12 years.

1.11 CONCLUSION

To summarize, this chapter has addressed the important question of leadership in organizations by first reviewing some definitions of quality and what they mean for the leader's attitudes and behaviour. Next, the origins and context of leadership were examined, in particular the differences said to exist between managing and leading. Special attention was also paid to why some quality management programmes fail, even when they are led by senior executives and driven by supposedly competent management. If crucial elements are omitted or not emphasized, the reasons must lie with the leaders (say, the gurus) and not with their followers.

Above all, the role of leaders at every level must be to critically reflect and assess the many offerings in the total quality market. Selecting the most appropriate may not necessarily be the most accessible or easily understood, or be the path which is easiest to follow. Perhaps the failure of quality programmes in many instances is testimony to the major tenet and slogan of quality itself: 'giving the customers what they want'. It may also be that leaders are guilty of collaboration here – as they are pressurized and time-conscious, they may be wanting quick solutions or easy-to-implement 'packages'. By all means, satisfy the customers, give them what they want, but help them make an informed choice first! This book is an attempt to do just that, and is built around the framework in Figure 1.4.

The reasoning underlying the framework is that the overall *strategy*

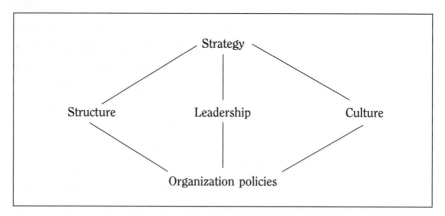

FIGURE 1.4   A context for leadership for quality

will determine the role that quality is to play and the *structure* will reflect how best the quality efforts may be organized. The *culture* will point to the values necessary: to choose and implement the strategy and make the structure workable. The *policies*, based on the values, will enable the organization to provide the necessary environment to deliver quality. Since it is *leadership* which will hold all this together, it is in the centre of the diagram.

In conclusion, the rationale for each chapter is as follows. Chapter 1 has taken an overview of quality and leadership. Chapter 2 emphasizes the strategic thinking that leaders can use to guide quality initiatives if they are to make a contribution to the effectiveness of the organization. Leaders at all levels need to position themselves and their units in relation to their overall organizational strategy. In Chapter 3, the structures necessary to deliver quality and their implications are reviewed. Next, the cultural aspects which can help or hinder quality programmes are examined in Chapter 4. To help embed the new ways of thinking and working, organizational policies need to be put in place to support them, and so these are the subject matter for Chapter 5.

While Chapters 2 to 5 cover the 'macro' aspects of leadership, setting it in context, the remaining chapters focus on the 'micro' elements, highlighting the more individual content of the leader's activities. Chapter 6 therefore examines one role of the leader, which is to face outwards towards customers, suppliers and stakeholders, making sure that the direction and practices of the organization are consistent with their expectations and ensuring high-quality standards and cost effectiveness.

The leader also has to face inwards, so in Chapter 7 the functions of the leader within the organization are discussed. In Chapter 8, there is a review of areas which the leader has to tackle in leading the change towards quality. Finally, Chapter 9 deals with the concerns and challenges which senior managers typically face with regard to quality and which will exercise their leadership skills.

ACTION QUESTIONS

- What styles of leadership are there in my organization?
- What implications do they have for quality?
- What role models are there which help or hinder quality improvement initiatives?

REFERENCES

1 Deming, W.E. (1986): *Out of the Crisis*, Cambridge University Press, Cambridge, UK.

2 Juran, J.M. (1989): *Juran on Leadership for Quality*, The Free Press, New York, USA.

3 Crosby, P.B. (1984): *Quality Without Tears*, McGraw-Hill, London, UK.

4 Oakland, J. (1989): *Total Quality Management*, Heinemann Professional, Oxford, UK.

5 Feigenbaum, A.V. (1991): *Total Quality Control*, McGraw-Hill, New York, USA.

6 Garvin, D.A. (1988): *Managing for Quality*, The Free Press, New York, USA.

7 Kano, N. (1984): 'Attractive Quality vs Must be Quality', *Hinshitsu* (Quality), **14** (2), pp. 39–48.

8 Clark, F.A. (1992): 'Quality and Service in the Public Sector', *Public Finance and Accounting*, 23 October, pp. 23–5.

9 Øvretveit, J. (1992): *Health Service Quality*, Blackwell, Oxford, UK.

10 Clark, F.A. (1992), op. cit.

11 Garvin, D.A. (1988) op. cit.

12 Drucker, P.F. (1992): *Managing for the Future*, Truman Talley Books, New York, USA.

13 Bennis, W. and Nanus, B. (1985): *Leaders*, Harper & Row, New York, USA.

14 Kotter, J.P. (1990): 'What Leaders Really Do', *Harvard Business Review*, **68** (3), pp. 103–11.

15 Burke, W.W. (1987): *Organization Development: A Normative View*, Addison Wesley, New York, USA.

16 Kelley, R.E. (1988): 'In Praise of Followers', *Harvard Business Review*, **66** (6), pp. 142–8.

17 Blake, R.R. and Mouton, J. (1964): *The Managerial Grid*, Gulf Publishing, Houston, Texas, USA.

18 Fiedler, F.E. (1967): *A Theory of Leadership Effectiveness*, McGraw-Hill, New York, USA.

19 Adair, J. (1984): *The Skills of Leadership*, Gower, Farnborough, UK.

20 Blanchard, K., Zigarmi, P. and Zigarmi, D. (1987): *Leadership and the One Minute Manager*, Fontana Collins, Glasgow, UK.

21 Szilagyi, A.D. (Jnr) and Schweiger, D.M. (1984): 'Matching managers to strategies: a review and suggested framework', *Academy of Management Review*, **9** (11), pp. 626–37.

22 *The Economist* (1992): 'The Cracks in Quality', April, pp. 85–6.

23 *Quality Today* (1989): 'What's Wrong With British Quality?', Feature, November, pp. 44–7.

24 *The Economist* (1992): *Making Quality Work – Lessons from Europe's Leading Companies*, EIU, London, UK.

25 Macdonald, J. (1993): 'Obsolete Absolutes', *Total Quality Management*, April, pp. 5–6.

26 *The Economist*, op. cit.

Strategic thinking for quality

2.1 INTRODUCTION

Increasingly, as top managers are becoming more involved with quality they are being expected to use it more as a strategic tool rather than merely as a way of making their organizations more efficient or delegating it to an individual or department to look after for compliance purposes. Not only is it viewed as differentiating an organization from the competition, but it may also be the first hurdle into some markets, or even the legitimization to operate at all.

As was pointed out in Chapter 1, leaders exist to create a vision and to shape, guide and ensure that strategy is executed and monitored. With quality programmes the requirement is still the same. Quality initiatives seem easier to implement fully when things are going well, but are easy to derail if there are cash-flow problems or insufficient revenue to cover fixed costs. The danger is that management may then wish to revert to the old hierarchical ways of decisions being made by the top level rather than by teams, and even retrench with extra control mechanisms and downsizing. These negate the long-term work of building in the benefits of quality. That is why the leader's primary responsibility is to make sure that quality is a strategic issue right from the very start, so that it can be planned in and, if necessary, refocused if resources are limited or immediate action needs to be taken.

Without clear strategic direction, quality programmes are unlikely to progress beyond the first stage of TQM, which is often more concerned with process and reporting, cost reduction, safety improvements and a more contented workforce. As the CEO of Florida Power and Light is quoted as saying[1]:

> This emphasis on process and format is typical of many organizations in the
> developmental stages of TQM. Unfortunately many companies never advance ...
> Our experience ... emphasizes the need to move promptly to the mature stage
> of TQM.

Clearly, a key task of strategic leadership is to judge when that point has
been reached.

One role of the strategic leader is to assess and interpret the
environment within which the organization operates. A useful framework[2]
within which to consider quality (although it was not originally designed for
that but for examining the power distributions affecting the market forces
in an industry) contains five elements: rivalry among organizations; buyer
power; supplier power; the threat of new substitutes; and the threat of new
entrants. These will now be expanded in relation to their implications for
quality.

2.2 CUT-THROAT COMPETITION

Within any industry there will be rivalry among organizations for
dominance, be it defined in terms of market share, growth rate, profitability
sales revenue or some other indicator. One way of achieving these ends is
through delivering high-quality products or services. Quality may be seen
not only as a means of differentiating organizations from the competition,
but also as the price of entry into a sector. In sectors based on trading in
commodities or less tangible services such as banking, insurance and
financial advice, it is the only way of signalling uniqueness to existing or
potential clients.

The importance of quality as a strategic weapon can be seen from the
following study. In one analysis of a database of some 3000 companies,[3]
quality not only separated successful ones from the competition, but did
indeed influence market share, reduce costs and increase profit margins.
Another study of the same database[4] concluded that:

> quality, defined as customers' evaluation of the business's product or service
> package compared to that of the competition, had a favourable impact on all
> measures of financial performance.

Businesses offering high-quality products or services tended to be more profitable than those of lower quality. Return on investment, profit as a percentage of sales, increased as quality increased. A remark attributed to Louis Gerstner Jnr, chairman and CEO of AMEX's travel-related services company, underlines its importance: 'It is our most strategic weapon. It is the only way we can differentiate our product in the market place.'

2.3 CONSUMER DEMANDS

One of the important pressures driving quality is the increasingly sophisticated consumers and customers. First, they want more than a fair price and reliable delivery of a product or service. Those aspects are taken for granted, and the trend then moves towards the more subjective aspects surrounding the good or service, such as reassurance or the ease of access to the organization. Secondly, they are now more likely to be aware of their choices. This is demonstrated in the proliferation of trade and other magazines which enable them to be more discerning about price, performance and other features, allowing detailed comparisons to be made. Thirdly, there are bodies dedicated to this end (such as *Which?* magazine) which seek out poor performers and publish the results of independent evaluations. Finally, independent watchdogs are set up to monitor and protect the needs of the customer. For example, the utilities in the UK have bodies such as Ofwat, Ofgas and Oftel for the water, gas and telecommunications industries respectively.

The information technology (IT) industry is a good example of a sector where buyers are insisting on higher quality. The case has been reported[5] of an electrical trading firm whose new warehousing system was said to be unable to cope with variations between 30-day and 31-day months. It is suing the supplier for £1.5 million, as its capacity to do business was seriously affected. The alleged reduction in quality was said to have had serious knock-on effects in areas such as credit freezing, management reporting and full audit trails.

Buyers acting independently or together are also able to 'dent' the image of quality which suppliers may falsely portray. In reaction to one company who priced software up to 200 per cent higher in the UK compared with the USA, one large and powerful customer made presentations on the subject to the trade press.[6] It was enough to ensure the required media exposure and a rethink by the firm. Some buyers, such as Nissan and Ford, are so powerful that they have their own codes of practice for what they require of their customers. Nissan Motor Manufacturing has 'The Nissan Way', and may send its staff on site to help the supplier conform to the required standard. In the same vein, Ford Motor Company has supplied some of its own computer-assisted design software to its suppliers to ensure that high-quality parts are produced. Finally, the chemicals giant ICI made sure that their carrier P&O had BS5750 accreditation before transporting their commodities and chemicals.

2.4 SUPPLIERS

Suppliers, too, have bargaining power, and developing a suitable business and working relationship with them is a key element in the maintenance of quality. The suppliers provide the raw materials for an organization. This can be interpreted in the widest sense: information or bookings as well as commodity products or partly finished goods – in fact, anything to which an organization adds value in some way. According to one source,[7] the purpose of managing the supply chain is:

> to achieve a balance between the goals of high customer service and a low inventory investment/low unit cost goals which are often seen as conflicting.

If any one activity fails, the chain of activities will be disrupted and service quality will be reduced.

It was further argued that the focus on the supply of resources is rarely at a strategic level, but usually only at an operational level. If supply issues are ignored by top management, then: 'there is imbalance, exploitable opportunities are missed and the impact of competitive threat is increased'. At a strategic level, it was maintained, the focus should be on:
- objectives and policies for the supply chain (responsiveness, product availability)
- the shape of the supply chain (facilities and locations)
- the organization's competitive package
- an outline organizational structure (bridging functional barriers and ensuring integration).

The need to focus at a strategic level and to ensure high quality has led to the encouragement of partnerships. For example, companies in the automotive industry have reduced the number of suppliers with whom they will do business and have developed very close links with companies (especially the Japanese) which are, in other respects, their competitors. The Rover–Honda link was just one such example prior to its takeover by BMW.

Partnership sourcing, as it is known, is a way of improving quality by getting close to the supplier and developing a long-term relationship. This involves knowing their business strategies, their markets, values and organization. The decision to follow this route must be a strategic one. There are important issues to be considered, such as sharing the risks associated with the supplier's delivery times, bad debts, cash flow and internal management. Will the chosen partner be reliable or, indeed, survive? Will the quality delivered be independent of fluctuations in costs? Then there are questions about whether the supplier is passing on cost reductions and its relative strength against other suppliers in the same sector. Is there a point at which the buyer integrates upstream through acquiring a supplier's business? Will the relationship with the supplier result in a key contribution to the organization maintaining its competitive edge? Thorough and wide-ranging investigations covering the operational details are necessary, but the balancing of the pros and cons can only be taken at the highest level.

If there are powerful buyers in the marketplace, then they can impose higher standards on the suppliers, thus driving up their own quality. In the retail sector, Marks and Spencer is renowned for its selectivity in its suppliers and will even offer training to ensure that there is an exact understanding of what is required. However, if the pressures become too severe, suppliers may attempt to regain power by joining forces (for example, on price) or by controlling their outlets (for example, by the use of authorized distributors).

When increased quality is the goal, the relationship has to be a long-term one. This must be the case when parties are committing themselves to make the investment worth while. This may be not only in the form of time, training for skills, money and management cooperation, but also in the sharing of research and development, new technology and understanding each other's core business and organization. A stable, long-term relationship enables both parties to have greater confidence in their mission.

It has been noted[8] that the new relationship will generate others, both at functional and hierarchical levels. This can be helpful in achieving cooperation, but it could make separation more difficult because of the complex web of interactions generated or the fact that disagreement about the effectiveness of an operation may not be shared by all the functions.

However, the closeness of these interdependencies may not be strong enough to prevent failure. Gaps in expectations may occur between the various parties. These may be in the areas of competence in technology, capability of the organization, culture and value systems. It is the last area which may constitute the largest stumbling block to integration and damage the ability of the supplier to deliver a high-quality service.

Suppliers may also be subject to political and environmental pressures which have an impact on quality. For example, the water industry in the UK, although privatized, has come under pressure from the EU to increase the quality of water over the next decade by raising the standards of treatment of waste water. This could result in suppliers increasing their prices if they have to conform.

2.5 NEW WAYS OF OFFERING THE PRODUCT OR SERVICE

It may be possible to provide a novel product or service merely by changing or acquiring a new supplier, but in other circumstances the drive may be internal. Companies are always seeking to be innovative and more cost-efficient in the way in which they offer their products or services. It is because of this very innovativeness that all the implications for quality cannot be seen in advance. Some of these may be detrimental and have implications for quality and customer satisfaction. Take, for example, the array of credit cards, cash cards and other forms of obtaining funds. While these have undoubtedly increased satisfaction for the customer regarding the flexibility and responsiveness of the services provided, they have also brought with them risks: unauthorized use of cards as a result of theft; siphoning of funds from accounts or debiting cardholders' accounts; a twilight business operation of providing information about creditworthiness and detailed descriptions of spending.

In today's world, the area of innovation may be one which merits the close attention of top management. In some sectors the life cycle of a product may be very short, so that there is continuous pressure to find new products or services. In the financial services sector a product may have a life of only three months, or in the IT software sector a release may only be viable for six months or less until a newer version is in place.

In the 'life cycle approach' to product launches, there is almost an expectation that minor problems will arise and that this is an acceptable customer risk. This philosophy is rampant in software releases, with the customer providing useful feedback to update the supplier. In a more closed loop situation[9] where all the major stakeholders (product developers, customers and allies) are involved, they may develop a coordinated approach to pre-launch and post-launch programmes. Strong leadership is therefore required at the product launch stage to choose which approach will have the best impact on quality and customer satisfaction.

2.6 NEW PLAYERS

Within an established industry sector there may be new entrants, which could upset the balance of power. The immediate and common problem is that the new entrant undercuts competitors through keen pricing. The others may respond in an effort to be competitive, while their quality suffers. Another risk is that the newcomer may have different quality standards (either higher or lower) compared with the rest of the industry. If the standard is lower, the industry's image may be tarnished by the maverick behaviour of the new player. Take, for example, the local high street. If one or two low-cost suppliers of clothing move in, others may follow and the high street starts to take on the appearance of a cut-price open air market. If standards are higher, this poses the threat of loss of market share, as there will be an inevitable time-lag for the remainder to catch up or close up. This has happened in many sectors both in the UK and worldwide as a result of Japanese competition. Cars, electrical goods and video technology are areas which, when the new entrants first offered their goods on the market, were described as shoddy, lacking in safety features and so on. One of the ways of keeping new players out is to maintain high quality because of the investment needed to ensure that the organization 'lives' quality. The message for organizational leaders here is that, when monitoring the environment, they need to examine the balance of these forces, note which have an impact on quality in their own organizations and those of their suppliers and distributors and make sure that they act in an appropriate way.

2.7 SURVIVAL IMPERATIVES

Apart from reading the environment, leaders need to emphasize the message that quality means survival. There is a telling quote in the context of quality and continuous improvement[10] which sums up the thinking of some of the West's international competition on its ability to survive:

> We asked him why Japanese companies had thrown open their factories and talked frankly about the secrets of their success. 'Because', he said, 'it would take you ten years to get to where we are now – and by that time we shall be even further ahead. And besides', he smiled, 'we know you won't do it.'

The timely strategic decisions on these matters therefore hold the key to survival. They may be reactive or proactive, but in either case they can transform the way in which organizations operate.

Reactive decisions to an organizational disaster (actual or potential) may trigger the strategic intention to use quality as a means of survival. The collapse of the banking arm of Johnson Matthey in the UK in the 1980s, and the pressure for improvement from Ford, a major customer to whom it supplied various metals, forced the company to adopt a total quality approach. Similarly, Paul Revere, the US insurance company, launched a 'Quality has Value' scheme as a result of its rapid decline in market share and pressure from its parent company.

Perhaps one of the most successful turnaround stories in this reactive mode is that of Rank Xerox. After ruling the photocopier market, profits were suddenly reduced from more than US$1 billion in 1980 to just US$6 million in 1981. This situation was plainly put by a senior member of the corporation:[11]

> Our survival as a company was at stake. We had to do something. We turned to quality to survive and it took a crisis to do it.

The crisis needed spelling out. At the time, it was estimated that the unit manufacturing cost equalled that of the Japanese US selling price which still included a healthy profit.

Even in proactive mode, the survival issue is at the forefront of organizational consciousness. The following two quotes[12] illustrate this. John Young, CEO of Hewlett Packard the computer systems manufacturer, is reported as saying: 'In today's competitive environment, ignoring quality is tantamount to committing corporate suicide.' In a similar vein, F. James McDonald, President of General Motors, reflects on their fortunes: 'If quality is not the number one operating priority at GM, there may be a time when there is no GM.'

It requires statements like these from leaders at the top of the organization to put quality on the managerial agenda, even when no immediate crisis is on the horizon.

There is another, less obvious survival imperative which is nevertheless significant. Increasingly, companies are developing new products, entering new markets or seeking to acquire complementary skills through joint ventures, alliances, franchise or other forms of cooperation. Each will want to satisfy itself about the reputation and quality of each other's offerings. Some partners will always be sought after; others will not, and this will reduce the viability and scope of their operations now and in the future.

At a more general level,[13] it has been said that organizations of the future need to be 'focused, fast, flexible and friendly' to survive. These are just the attributes that an organization based on quality is said to offer through its philosophy, structure and management style which are targeted on continuous improvement, underpinned by the willingness and ability to learn.

Perhaps the last word on all this should be that attributed to Deming, the quality guru, on the implementation of his quality philosophy: 'You do not have to do these things; survival is not compulsory.'

2.8 GOVERNMENT MANDATES

Leaders need to assess the strategic implications for quality of governments not only in the UK but worldwide, since they are increasingly affecting quality standards through their mandates. These are the externally given terms of reference within which organizations have to operate. They can appear in various forms: legislation, charters, articles of association or ministerial statements, and set out those things that organizations should or should not do. They are fixed in the short term, but may change over time and have an impact both through regulatory and deregulatory measures. How organizations deal with them is a matter for strategic concern. Keeping close to their thinking is a function of senior management, and in one telecommunications company it is deemed to be a competence at that level.

Regulatory aspects can cover environment, health, safety, building regulations, consumer protection and a host of other areas affecting daily life. The public sector, for example, has been required to implement market testing (as a way of ensuring that the highest standards are obtained for services which it is currently providing) and competitive tendering to see that the best value for money is obtained. This has led to radical overhauls within the civil service departments and local authorities. These have had to define their core businesses more accurately and develop methodologies for evaluating in-house activities such as staffing, costs and service quality and improving quality specifications. As for the firms themselves, they may lobby various government departments for general rules which may be to their advantage.

Deregulation of services in the financial services sector, airlines and utilities has also affected service quality. Competition has increased the variety of offerings and non-essentials surrounding the services. For example, airlines not only have varying classes of service but will offer theatre bookings in another city and a taxi service to complete the journey. In the USA, government interventions in the form of the US Federal Trade Commission are reported[14] to have affected how industries operate, insisting that manufacturers are responsible for failures even though they may occur just after the warranties expire. The Federal Trade Commission may file complaints if the product has systematic, known defects; if the company could have disclosed information to buyers about likely problems but failed to do so; and if the agency sees action to be in the public interest and likely to increase consumer welfare. The effect of intervention is to deter shoddy goods since it increases the cost of expensive defects which need rectification or replacement.

In Japan, the Ministry of International Trade and Industry (MITI) has in the past commanded loyalty from most businesspeople through subsidies, protection from competition and the expression of displeasure if guidelines were not followed. Yet in retrospect this can be seen to have had limited success in industries such as chip technology (where technologies diverged) or in petrochemicals where plants were substandard and over-staffed). It also realized that the venture capital needed for innovation and continuous improvement would not be forthcoming in an over-regulated financial services sector. Leadership has a key role to play here, both in protecting the organization from unwanted, over-expensive bureaucracy or interference in the regulatory area and from the mavericks in a deregulated environment. Those involved in leading quality at every level have to be very attuned to what is going on outside the organization and to communicate this quickly to staff.

2.9 CHARACTERISTICS OF A STRATEGIC APPROACH TO QUALITY

Once the environment has been mapped, the starting point for a strategic approach to quality is a statement or restatement of the organization's purpose and values. It is against this background that the overall strategy can be devised and the contribution that quality can make to an organization can be assessed. Mission and values will be discussed in more detail in Chapter 4, because of their impact on organizational culture.

There are several reasons why quality has been on the agenda for strategic thinking. Unacceptable quality leads to[15]:

- loss of reputation
- loss of market share
- loss of profitability
- reduced ability to deal with foreign competition
- increases in liability suits
- increasing government scrutiny.

There were many examples in the USA which triggered a need for action. In particular, the semiconductor industry in the 1980s was shocked to learn that Japanese chips had a zero failure rate at incoming inspection which could not be equalled by the leading US manufacturers.

Many external forces (mentioned in this and earlier sections), either singly or together, may shape top management's attitudes to quality because of their impact on strategy. The need for senior management to stress the importance of quality within their organizations has been highlighted elsewhere[16]:

Nor could it [quality] be relegated to lower levels of the organization, where functional loyalties might interfere with a broader strategic vision.

This does not deny the necessity of operational involvement for quality to succeed, but it does emphasize the requirement to rise above internal rivalry which might exist for a variety of structural reasons. It puts quality very firmly in the remit of senior managers because of the unique perspective they can bring to oversee the effects of various initiatives and their ability to look outside as well as inside their organizations.

For a view of quality to be strategic, it must focus first and foremost on the customer and the comparative standards of performance of competitors for that particular organization and industry. According to one view,[17] a strategic approach needs to be:

- defined from the customer's point of view
- linked with profitability
- used as a competitive weapon
- linked with strategic planning
- given organization-wide commitment.

These points need expansion and will now be taken in turn to assess their contribution to strategic thinking.

Customer's viewpoint

In the past, quality was often defined by the internal standards of quality assurance and quality control. Now the standard has become externally derived. Quality is what the customer perceives it to be, not what organizations would like him or her to perceive or something that can be measured in an idealized or absolute state. To adopt this perspective means getting very close to the customer to identify requirements. This can only be done if quality is broken down into dimensions which he or she sees as relevant. However, what is important to customers changes over time (Fig. 2.1).

Royal Mail has a number of key indicators of customer satisfaction with which it monitors performance. It has noted that, as quality improves, one of the indicators may 'drop off' the list as either customers become accustomed to superior performance or it no longer features highly for other reasons. Moreover, some may have difficulty in communicating what they actually want. This may be the case in the services sector. For example,

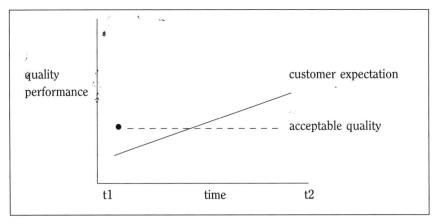

FIGURE 2.1   Expectations and quality

from the IT specialist's viewpoint, the problem is that the customer or end user cannot easily specify what is wanted and may be unaware of, or not understand, the technological possibilities which might deliver the end results. These service gaps can only be bridged by constant dialogue.

In fact, the services sector has a number of different characteristics which make it more difficult to assess and deliver quality. These are, according to one authority[18]:

- *intangibility* (cannot easily measure it or evaluate it in advance of purchase);
- *production and consumption are inseparable* (depends on provider-buyer interaction and quality control is difficult to achieve);
- *variability of resources* (performance is difficult to standardize);
- *perishability* (cannot store yesterday's beds, rooms, operations, consultations against future demand);
- *ownership* (buying a service does not result in ownership, only access or usage).

In reality, most services are a mixture of tangibles and intangibles, such as food served on an airline. Evaluation of the service is thus highly dependent on people's perceptions of delivery rather than on absolute and visible criteria.

It has been pointed out[19] that there are different ways of looking at service quality:

- *the technical quality of the outcome of the service encounter* (what the customer receives);

- *the functional quality of the process itself* (how the service is provided and is concerned with the psychological interaction of the buyer and the seller);
- *the corporate image dimension of quality* (which is the result of how consumers perceive the firm and can be expected to be built up mainly through the technical and functional quality. A further distinction was also made in the concept of a service product (which is related to service quality);
- *a basic service package* (a core service with a facilitating support service);
- *an augmented service* (the service process and the customer's participation in the process and interactions between company and customers).

In the public sector (which is itself exceedingly diverse) the intention to deliver a high-quality service may be constrained by a number of contradictions related to the customer and the context of the service which have been identified by the author[20]:

- *customer identity* (who is/are the customer(s)?)
- *harmony of goals* (do the customers have different goals from each other?)
- *permanence* (are the customers permanent, elected, appointed, individuals, committees and so on?)
- *power* (to whom are the service providers accountable?)
- *worker's commitment* (full-time, part-time, paid, unpaid?)
- *performance criteria* (budget, profit, surplus, breakeven?)
- *diverse values* (many subcultures within one organization, each with a long history and tradition).

These things, either singly or in combination, can make quality and service difficult to deliver here. The answers to apparently simple questions of customer goals, permanence, power, commitment, performance and values provide a complex context for the delivery of quality in service operations.

Profitability

The second strategic link is that quality and profitability are related in different ways. First, perhaps after some initial expenditure such as training, quality improves and the result is lower costs. The rationale is that reducing the costs of poor quality drives down the costs of doing business. Margins between operating costs and revenue can increase without even having to gain additional revenue. Secondly, the analysis of the Profit Impact on Market Strategy (PIMS) database of companies which operate primarily in North American and European markets demonstrates that quality is related to market share. Businesses offering better quality were shown to have the following benefits:

- stronger customer loyalty
- more repeat purchases
- less vulnerability to price competition
- ability to command a higher relative price without adversely affecting market share.

Taken together, these reasons provide a very powerful incentive for investing in quality initiatives. In the words of Jack Welch, chairman of General Electric in 1990:

> Quality is the best way of assuring customer loyalty; it is our best defence against foreign competition and the only way to secure continuing growth and profits.

One study[21] on the PIMS database showed that, as the relative quality index achieved by companies rose, so did the return on investment (ROI). In a group with low quality, less than a quarter had an ROI greater than 25 per cent. By contrast, 60 per cent of the businesses in the high-quality group achieved this. A further analysis demonstrated the reasons for this finding, confirming what managers intuitively believe: higher quality businesses tend to command higher prices than those of their competitors. They conclude on this point that:

> Quality itself drives profit, not price and those businesses with high prices but low quality do rather poorly, while businesses reporting high quality without premium prices do as well as those with premium priced quality.

The reasoning offered is that a combination of high price and lower quality will ultimately lose market share and, conversely, high quality and lower price will gain it.

Quality as a competitive weapon

Thirdly, at a strategic level, a quality organization means being the leading provider of goods and services, fending off the competition or, at the very minimal level, having the licence to do business at all. If consumer expectations rise in a generally upward direction, then today's competitive weapon can evaporate before the year is out, so there has to be a continual anticipation of, and search for, what is going to be an effective quality platform for the organization. British Telecom has a post of competitor analyst and runs a competitor newsline. This is where existing staff, who may have a great deal of contact with customers, may hear much news about competitors and can telephone to a central point with their information.

At the Xerox Corporation in the 1980s, quality was the way the company chose to recover its position in the marketplace, lost to the Japanese competition. British Airways also used quality in its 'Putting People First' campaign to transform itself from a loss-maker in the early 1980s to a profit of some £200 million at the end of the decade.

In a similar strategic situation, quality was used as a competitive weapon by Hewlett Packard, the hi-tech scientific/computing instruments company. Faced with the demands for higher-quality products from its customers and the threat of their migration to the competition, retaining market share was its number one priority, and superior quality the vehicle to deliver it.

Two generic strategies for achieving success in beating the competition have been identified.[22] One is to obtain the overall cost leadership within an industry. The other is to differentiate oneself from the competition to achieve a superior position from the customer's perspective. The same author noted that these two strategies were rarely combined, but that it was possible by focusing on a particular market segment. Daimler Benz concentrated on the luxury market and was able to maintain low cost and perceived quality advantage over its competitors. Cost reduction strategies, according to one leading authority,[23] have merely resulted in price reduction, so that there are no real winners among the suppliers. This has led companies to follow the quality route as a way of generating higher returns.

In a survey of some 600 retailers in the USA[24] (sportswear chains, department stores, etc.), it was found that there was a marked preference for doing business with quality service providers. Some 60 elements were identified which could have an impact on market share. Nine critical elements were shown to have a significant impact on market share, five of which were service attributes (order fill, delivery consistency, order accuracy, responsiveness to customers, problem-solving helpfulness) as opposed to product attributes or value attributes (credit terms).

Strategic planning link

The fourth criterion which has to be met for quality to be considered as a strategic weapon is planning. To deliver quality, effective behaviour has to be planned in at the highest level, not delegated to some functional department or group thought to have the time to look after it. British Telecom's initial programme was a long-term initiative involving massive restructuring. Similarly, the British Airways quality programme begun in 1983 is always being updated with new initiatives. The objective of reducing field failure rates of products at Hewlett Packard was planned to be achieved over ten years. Results do not come quickly, and a long-term perspective is vital to see the programme through its initial stages. However, this does not mean that milestones cannot be placed at key points along the journey.

Quality and organization-wide commitment

The concept of the internal customer has to become ingrained in the corporate thinking before quality can succeed. This means that everyone in the organization must assume responsibility for quality, with top management taking a strong and visible role. The remit of the quality professional in strategic quality management is therefore not to take total ownership of quality. However, it does involve creating awareness, educating, training, goal setting and collaborating with departments across traditional functional and organizational boundaries.

2.10 NICHE STRATEGIES

While knowing the general characteristics of a strategic perspective that an organization needs to have before it can deliver quality is imperative, it does not indicate where it needs to direct its efforts. That can only be done by everyone adopting the first criterion of being customer-focused. The phrase

Performance	primary operating characteristics of the product
Features	secondary aspect or desirables
Reliability	likelihood of the product malfunctioning or failing within a specified time period
Conformance	the extent to which the product's design and operating characteristics meet the necessary standards
Durability	the life of the product
Serviceability	speed, courtesy, competence and ease of repair
Aesthetics	subjective assessments of the overall appeal of the product: aesthetics, fit, feel, finish, smell
Perceived quality	an overall assessment of the product's quality and its reputation

FIGURE 2.2   Eight dimensions of quality

'close to the customer' means more than staying in touch or responding to requests. The critical question to ask is: 'How does my organization add value to theirs?' One of the 'best practice' tips from a government publication[25] says: 'Ask your customers what your core business is; they may recognise and value qualities you can't see.'

Asking the customer directly is a way of translating the overall strategy into a more focused niche strategy. One method[26] proposed a strategic model for quality by separating the concept into eight distinct categories or dimensions, each reflecting a separate facet of what the customer may want. Figure 2.2 summarizes the meaning of these dimensions.

By this process of disaggregation, an organization could then determine which dimensions were most suitable for its specific product and how it might compete in the marketplace using those dimensions. The organization could select which dimensions to use as competitive weapons. However, this would also depend on the market conditions, what the customers wanted and what the organization's competitors were doing. During the late 1970s and early 1980s the Japanese motor industry built up a good reputation for its cars based on their reliability and their finish. Thirty or so years ago, Japanese cars had a poor safety record and a tendency to rust. The industry decided to compete on two particular dimensions not strongly represented by Western manufacturers but for which they sensed there was an underlying demand: aesthetics and reliability. This focus paid off in their rapid growth of market share in most

Western countries. These dimensions of quality are now considered in more detail below.

A product's *performance* is the basic operating characteristics, for example, the acceleration of a car or the punctuality of an airline. These are the common reasons for purchasing a product. They are usually the measurable attributes which can then be rated to compare the performance of different products.

The *features* of a product are the additional, rather than the essential, operating characteristics found in the previous category. They are the optional extras which are not crucial to the use of the product but may give added enjoyment to the user. Some executive cars are respected for features such as walnut fascias and leather seats which are almost essential aspects of image making. Examples of other features are free drinks on airline flights or stereo sound on televisions. It is important for an organization to be clear about which are the primary and which are the secondary aspects of its products. This means objectively investigating the customer's needs to ensure that all the performance factors are met.

Just how *reliable* a product is is demonstrated by the likelihood of its failure within a certain time period. Common measures for durable products are mean time to first failure and mean time between failures. However, the nature of these measures makes them less appropriate for goods or services which are produced and consumed almost simultaneously. Increasingly, failure rates are becoming a more important element in the buying decision. The costs of a failed product and associated preventative maintenance may represent a substantial proportion of the overall product cost, quite apart from its original purchase price.

As a product characteristic, *conformance* assesses how well the product meets the standards set. These are normally based on parameters related to engineering and are measured as deviations from a specified target, often within an acceptable range. A well-publicized example of a conformance target is that adopted by Motorola. Its 'Six Sigma' quality goal specifies only 3.4 defects per million opportunities or 99.999 per cent defect-free manufacturing.[27] An important part of setting the initial requirement for conformance, however, is meeting all the design and operating characteristics that customers want and its performance as specified by them.

The *durability* of a product refers to its lifespan and the degree of usage which one might reasonably expect from it. For example, televisions would be compared on the number of hours they would last. Measuring the durability of a product is now much more than just considering the lifespan; it may also include other factors such as the ease and cost of maintenance and the cost of the model. This would then be assessed against the cost of a more durable model in the first place. The latter might be more expensive initially, but have fewer running costs over the longer term. The simplified construction of the TV set over the years is an example of this. Since durability and reliability are connected, many suppliers offer lifetime guarantees on their products: for example, Scotch offer one on their videotapes.

If failure in a product occurs, repairs may be necessary. The product's *serviceability* covers the speed, courtesy, competence and ease of repair and the associated staff support. How acceptable the standards are varies according to individual needs. Customers may decide to wait only a specific period of time for repairs, especially if the product is critical to a business or has safety or 'life or death' implications.

The *aesthetics* of a product may also be a very powerful element in the decision to buy. These are very subjective judgements and depend on the personal appreciation of many elements. Nevertheless, how the product looks, feels, sounds, tastes or even smells to the customer can still be measured. Even though this depends on individual preferences, the elements can still be rated in these highly subjective areas, and statistical techniques also exist to examine the power of different combinations of features.

The last element is that of *perceived quality*. When deciding to buy a product, an individual may not have all the necessary information and so will use indirect ways of making a judgement based on tangible and intangible factors. Public image and advertising and the brand name of the product contribute to a reputation which will help the consumer come to a view about the product's quality. For example, many products which are made in Japan are often thought to be of a much higher quality than those of their Western competitors just because of Japan's reputation for building high-quality products. Perceived quality may also be enhanced by endorsements or referrals (such as those given for safety and security products recommended by former high-ranking police or fire officers).

To summarize, these dimensions appear more suited to hard products than to the more intangible aspects associated with services. This is not surprising, since these eight dimensions were originally derived from a study of the air conditioning manufacturing sector in the USA. However, 'service' was later added[28] as another dimension for satisfying the customer, but this is not the whole answer since service can itself be disaggregated.

Other research[29] has indicated that many dimensions are not covered by the Harvard Business School's classification. These have been listed and expanded elsewhere[30]:

- *knowing the customer* (really understanding his or her needs, not making assumptions);
- *responsiveness* (willingness of employees to provide the product or service);
- *access* (approachability and ease of contact with the organization from the customer's point of view);
- *security* (freedom from danger, risk or doubt relating to the product or service);
- *credibility* (trustworthiness, believability and honesty of the organization);
- *courtesy* (politeness, respect, consideration, friendliness of contact personnel from the customer's point of view);
- *communication* (keeping customers informed in language they can understand and listening to them);
- *competence* (possession of the required skills and knowledge to produce the product or service).

These two lists taken together provide many possible dimensions on which to compete. Another similar approach to the service industries sector has been developed[31] which refined many dimensions down to five key ones (Fig. 2.3).

These dimensions are useful as they are the ones on which customers can assess a wide range of service industries. They are the special areas for differentiation from which goals and objectives must flow and around which an organization's strategies are built.

Finally, perceived quality depends on the criteria which customers apply to value. Relative value has been conceptualized[32] as quality divided by price. Preferences are set by the value, that is, the perceived quality/price ratio of one product in relation to another. The rivalry between airlines is a good illustration of this, as they compete on low fares. The

Tangibles	physical facilities, equipment and appearance of personnel
Reliability	ability to perform the promised service dependably and accurately
Responsiveness	willing to help customers and provide prompt services
Assurance	knowledge and courtesy of employees and their ability to convey trust and knowledge
Empathy	caring, individual attention that the firm provides for its customers

FIGURE 2.3   Five dimensions of service quality

pricing policy of BA in the summer of 1993 as a means of sharpening competition in the USA resulted in US airlines cutting domestic fares by up to 30 per cent to increase late summer traffic. Then, Northwest Airlines, American and Delta all joined in the fray.

In fact, it has been shown[33] that beating the competition on quality is a more likely way to gain market share than trying to win a price war. Choosing cost cutting over customer-perceived quality is not a sound strategy. For example, lower market price is usually matched by a competitor, especially if the products are not differentiated, resulting in the same share but less revenue. However, improved quality is more difficult to instigate, as competitors need time, money and innovation to catch up. Superior quality allows the organization to maintain a high value position in the short term and to hold onto it in the long term. However, this needs monitoring and auditing.

2.11 AUDIT

Identifying niche strategies on which to compete and the commitment to quality at a strategic level is a fundamental starting point for change. However, before any action can follow it is important to conduct a critical audit of the organization's current environmental situation and its influence on quality from design to delivery. Included in the audit will be the resources necessary to ensure quality at each stage: human, technical, financial, materials and accommodation for staff. It will also include policies and processes and some of the less tangible aspects of organizational life which may be difficult to measure (Chapter 4, 4.8). Nevertheless, they may have a major impact on quality and there are a number which are usually assessed: organizational culture; management style; employee commitment and satisfaction (for example, IBM's annual staff survey or Royal Mail's rolling quarterly one so that all 165 000 staff are covered) ; and the learning capability of its people. The audit will also examine these in relation to various indices of customer satisfaction. For example, BT's programme for quality involved conducting monthly surveys of public opinion to understand customers' perceptions of, and satisfaction with, BT's service. For Royal Mail, records of customer complaints are another barometer of their opinion (see Chapter 3, 3.8).

Three major reasons for conducting a quality audit[34] have been identified: survival, compliance and credibility. First, if the organization is unable to assess its own performance its business could be taken over by another or decisions made which could affect its future. The operating parallel in the public sector would be that funding would be withheld or the business contracted out. This is demonstrated in the market testing philosophy of the civil service, local authority and health services. Secondly, the regulatory environment is complex and becoming more so, especially in the financial services and telecommunications sector, and in order to survive the organization must be able to produce evidence of compliance. Therefore the relevant data require systematic gathering to predetermined standards via some form of audit. Thirdly, if an organization does not conduct its own quality audit, others will do so (by formally or informally noting errors and omissions). Their reports, perhaps based on false information and hearsay, may be inaccurate or counterproductive and therefore affect the organization's reputation and mission. For an audit to be effective, the starting point must be to ask the question: 'What would your customers (internal and external) want to achieve with your audit?'

A convenient classification[35] of an organization's approach to a quality audit is given below:

- *product audit* (of the finished product/paperwork)
- *process audit* (of an activity to check that inputs conform to requirements)
- *internal systems audit* (of the internal management controls)
- *external systems audit* (of the control of external relations with contractors, vendors and suppliers).

While all these areas provide a good basis from which to start, they omit the areas of finance, environment and culture which are crucial to an organization's operation and affect the commitment and level of quality which is to be achieved. To be effective, all these aspects need to be considered together, along with the industry and competitor analysis outlined at the beginning of the chapter. Despite all this, audits are not a sufficient mechanism to ensure quality. Comparative research on the superior and lower performers[36] in a number of different plants in the air conditioning industry showed that: 'Superior quality is associated with well defined management practices and not simply a supportive culture.'

Leadership is vital to supporting the audit process in the organization.

2.12 CLARIFYING THE CORPORATE OBJECTIVES

One of the reasons why quality programmes may not deliver benefits to an organization is that the overall corporate objectives may not be clear. For example, in a rapidly changing environment, or in a subsidiary of a larger company, senior management may find that, if they have not given the matter sufficient importance, boundaries may become blurred and accountabilities governed by politics rather than by the demands of the business. The chairman and CEO of Florida Power and Light is on record[37] as saying that a change in external environment resulted in the need for a downsized organization and that it presents no impediment to the practice of TQM.

Adopting a quality management philosophy before focusing on the customer can lead to the use of fashionable distractions such as empowerment, teamwork and quality circles. On their own, they are general concepts which, without goal direction, are limited in the value they can add to the corporate objectives. According to the corporate quality officer at CIBA-Geigy Ltd, the Swiss-based chemical multinational[38]:

> CIBA believes that a company must first have a vision and clear strategic direction. TQM is one of the tools to achieve the goals arising from this vision.

The importance of having corporate objectives is illustrated by the former CEO of ITT, Harold S. Geenen.[39] The existence of management inattention to quality results from the priority of the given objectives, especially those with a focus on short-term results and their respective sanctions:

> Operating managers know they cannot get into deep trouble for creating non-conformance products or services. They will be frowned upon for these difficulties but they can really be put down for profit loss. Therefore they concentrate on financial and schedule matters. Quality is third.

All this points to the need for leaders to show how quality is integrated with the business.

2.13 ALIGNING QUALITY GOALS WITH STRATEGIC GOALS

An interesting case of alignment of strategic goals with quality goals was seen with Honda's reaction to loss of sales early in 1993. Instead of laying off staff, which could have damaged morale and led to a lowering of quality in the manufacturing process, it chose to channel its energies differently. It taught its 10 000 non-union staff how to maintain and repair their own machines so that stoppages on the line would become a thing of the past. This is the sort of tactic that can impact directly on profitability.

The previous section covered the need to have a niche strategy. One of the reasons why quality initiatives fail is that their goals may not be aligned with the strategic goals of the organization in terms of financing, resourcing, timing or what they are expected to deliver. A requirement to increase sales turnover can be achieved as easily by acquisition as by increasing market share through improved quality. Downsizing (if by means other than natural wastage or voluntary retirement) after a quality drive only increases scepticism. A quality programme superimposed on poor systems and structures is doomed from the start, and quality used merely as a means of rooting out inefficiencies has little chance of survival. These kinds of 'knee jerk' reaction signal to employees that not only has quality not been aligned to strategy, but that there was probably no strategy in the first place.

Scandinavian Airline System (SAS) was determined to become a customer-oriented company. It was losing US$20 million per annum. The company used to treat all expenses as an evil until it decided that 'They could give a competitive edge if they contributed to our goal of serving the business customer.'[40]

Every procedure and resource was scrutinized against this goal. The result was a strategic plan for revitalizing the company. This meant investing an additional US$45 million and increasing operating expenses by US$12 million a year for 147 different projects (for example, a punctuality campaign, service courses for 12 000 staff and so on). In the words of the CEO Jan Carlzon:

> We had no guarantee that these additional expenses would bring in more revenue. But it was also our only chance because the option of reducing costs had already been used.

However, while investing the US$45 million, the company found that other procedures and policies were not making a contribution to the goal of serving business customers. These cuts were therefore simple to spot, and, by definition, SAS could see that they would not harm the company's goals. They resulted in savings of US$40. This example illustrates the leadership role of the president in being able to calculate the strategic payoff.

2.14 COSTS OF QUALITY AND STRATEGIC PAYOFF

Poor quality may increase the cost of delivering a product or service and, conversely, high quality may reduce costs through the minimization of error, wastage and duplication of effort. The former chairman of the Chrysler Corporation, Lee Iacocca, is reputed to have remarked that every fourth worker was an unnecessary cost as that worker was merely being paid for putting right errors made by the other three! Historically, the costs of quality have been broken down into three main areas (which can be further refined according to need): prevention, appraisal, internal failure and external failure. This can be illustrated by the story of the Leyland-Daf component which cost £1 to purchase. Had it been noted on receipt, it could have been returned at cost price. After machining, its value had been increased to £6, and to £36 when in a subassembly for a truck. Had the error been spotted at the appraisal stage, the internal failure costs would not have risen to £96 when the subassembly was built into a truck. Failure in the field meant that it cost £870 to replace, along with the customer goodwill and damage to corporate image.

According to one source[41]: 'Firms often do not calculate the costs of quality but those that do often find the results are startling.'

The same author continues by providing some striking examples:

- Half of all the annual cheque processing costs in US banks are a result of faulty cheques.
- Firestone's recall of radial tyres one year cost US$135 million (more than the firm's net income for that year).
- IBM reckoned that 25 per cent of manufacturing and administrative time is normally spent on the repair of defects and errors; eliminating these problems could increase output by more than 25 per cent.

Companies who provide high-quality products and services may also be found at the top of their industries in terms of financial indicators: Hewlett Packard, Procter and Gamble and Johnson and Johnson. Applying quality management methods, Corning Glass turned around its television glass business, and over three years its product specifications improved by 40 per cent; output by 20 per cent; and reduced dimensional variability by 17 per cent. AT&T used a teamwork approach to design a line carrier for manufacturability. In the first two years of the product's life only two design changes were needed, compared with a successful earlier product which needed 24; warranty costs dropped to 2 per cent of the original.

However, whereas the above examples and earlier references to the PIMS database reinforce this view of quality, care needs to be taken when making predictions about the strategic implications.[42] The argument is as follows: if taking a high perceived quality position were the easy way to high profits, newer firms would enter at the quality end of the market and erode profits down to a normal level. There must be some entry barrier which prevents this mechanism from working. An organization must therefore be sure that it does not have to overcome a barrier higher than everyone else's.

Over-emphasis on the costs of quality can have potentially detrimental effects. With a very large organization in terms of the number of employees and size of turnover, estimating the cost of poor quality and then allocating it to various business groups as theirs to reduce, can be demoralizing. Royal Mail decided against such actions as it would have meant that certain parts of the organization would have to 'carry' a very high load over which they did not have total control. Furthermore, it decided that there might not be many benefits in keeping a running total of costs of quality, since the effort involved in collating data would be too time-consuming for an organization of its size. As a general point, the ideal situation of being able to assess the costs of quality precisely may not be practicable for a variety of reasons: lack of detailed records; inflexible accounting systems; confidentiality; and the difficulty of attribution.

Even if the costs of quality could be adequately captured by traditional accounting systems, there are other considerations. For example, maintaining current relationships with suppliers involves time, effort and financial costs additional to a current business contract. A climate of trust may be easily eroded through mistakes, incorrect documentation, invalid information or failure to deliver a service. Opportunity costs also arise from poor quality. For example, it may affect the ability to command a price above the market norm if poor service is a result of poor relationships with suppliers. Then there is the actual or potential loss of customers, since dissatisfied customers tell, on average, another ten. Even if customers are retained, there are the associated costs of handling complaints, offering direct or indirect compensation and general goodwill. Therefore the costs of quality have to be examined in a broader context than previously may have been the case, in particular by senior management and the board.

2.15 THE ROLE OF THE BOARD

From research conducted over the last 25 years, three sets of interrelated roles played by boards have been identified[43]: service, strategy and control. Service activities include representation of the organization's interest in the community, linking it with the external environment and ceremonial roles (shareholders' meetings and special functions). These activities serve to weld the organization's identity and reputation, its mission and prestige in the community. The strategic role involves defining the firm's core business, developing its mission and guiding its strategy. Directors increase their firm's competitive position by focusing on specific goals and strategies. Corporate control requires the selection of senior executives, monitoring and evaluation of performance and alignment of their interests to ensure shareholders' satisfaction.

Any board is accountable to its key stakeholders and represents the organization's affairs in a legal context. The strategic payoff of quality programmes should therefore be carefully considered as a major concern, since quality initiatives may require proportionately large investments of time, effort and resources and will affect the organization's deliverables in both the short and long term.

Once directors have satisfied themselves about the strategic payoff of quality, they can contribute by ensuring that the mission and values of the organization (which will affect the delivery of quality) are actually in place, are consistent and are communicated effectively inside and outside the organization. The position and multiple roles of board directors give them plenty of scope to influence the take-up of quality if they are so inclined:

- *selection of the CEO and senior executives* (Are they committed to quality? Do they have a track record in change programmes?)
- *monitoring and evaluating senior executives' performance* (Is a quality component built into the process?)
- *protection of shareholders' interests* (Do they understand what best practice in quality looks like and the acceptability of the returns?)
- *commitment of resources* (Do they recognize the full extent of the commitment and are they willing to back it? Royal Mail allocated £2 million to training at the start of its programme.)
- *adjusting compensation packages* (Do they reflect improvement on the key performance measures for quality?)
- *maintaining or raising the prestige profile in the community* (Do they attract good publicity about quality?)
- *enhancement of the organization's capacity to raise funds* (Are they active in broadcasting the benefits of quality to their organization's performance?)
- *dealing with threats in the external environment* (Are they able to contain them so that internal work on quality is not destroyed, as could have happened with BA over its unfair practice allegations by Virgin Atlantic?)

More specifically, a survey[44] of very experienced, senior, non-executive directors found that, in a third of the appointments, the role they were expected to play was not clearly defined. Only half were backed up with a clear contract. There is therefore plenty of scope for them to shape their role and contribution to quality.

Much of the time a board is supplied with information which is aggregated, summarized or highlighted in some form. This can sometimes remove the urgency or emotionality contained in employees' or customers' feelings and how they are being treated, or the uncertainty which is being created by high-level deliberations in the company. The Nationwide Building Society[45] has a 'Talkback' process, where a sample of the workforce can 'cross-examine' directors and senior managers without going through their own line management. This process was initiated as a response to low morale and uncertainty about the future. To aid the internal process, videos of the local meetings were made, including coverage of the most difficult questions. This encouraged viewers to see that they were allowed to ask searching questions. The first series of meetings at 14 venues drew around 100 people, representing more than 10 per cent of the workforce. The internal company newspaper also reported question and answer sessions, and in just over a year around one-sixth of the workforce has been covered, with more meetings planned.

Other companies seek to establish closer ties with the staff in order to hear any views at first hand. The managing director of Cable and Wireless, James Ross, has allocated certain days for 'phone-ins' from different business regions and companies on which he will personally be available to take calls. Marks and Spencer, too, is renowned for its directors' involvement through their spot checks on stores. In fact, in a book about non-profit organizations[46], one view expressed is that board members should 'meddle' – that is to say, they should be interested, know about programmes, understand people, and care. Non-profit organizations, it is said, tend to be organized so that 'meddling' is part of the job. Members sit on committees dealing with issues which force them to collaborate directly with those working in the particular area of concern. The caveat here is that 'constructive meddling' is required: it must strengthen, not divide, an organization. Therefore the CEO needs to be kept informed. A staff member must report any contact immediately and in writing to the CEO and copy it to the board member concerned.

2.16 SELLING QUALITY TO THE TOP TEAM

Even though the board may stand behind the quality efforts, it is vital to sell quality to the top team. Quality management is a philosophy and a set of guiding principles which constitute the foundation for continuous improvement. Acceptance of that philosophy is vital, but can easily be distorted by the techniques associated with its implementation masquerading as quality itself. Secondly, there is a tendency to go for the major quality problems in a company, which means that implementation often comes with a high 'up-front' investment, with perhaps little to show for it for up to three years. This requires both an act of faith on the part of the top team and reinforcement with examples of success. Their interest will be aroused if quality can be related to the customer and the competitive position of the organization. The benefits of quality can only be assessed in relation to that part of the overall strategy which they were designed to fulfil.

It is therefore crucial to be quite clear what the quality initiative is designed to achieve, both as part of the strategic plan and as a separate stand-alone change programme. The typical business benefits associated with quality are listed below:

- increased customer loyalty and repeat purchases
- less vulnerability to price and decrease in marketing costs
- increase in market share and a customer referral system
- reduction in waste and rework and less work in progress
- reduced failure in the field and lower warranty costs
- reduced costs of litigation, fewer complaints and staff needed to handle them
- recoup of initial investment in attracting the customer.

Senior managers, however, are more convinced by 'big name' companies than by generalities, and some are given below:

- Barclaycard quality programmes are estimated to produce benefits worth £20 million per year.
- GEC-Plessey Communications reduced equipment returns by 90 per cent, scrap costs by 75 per cent and doubled output over five years.
- ICL reduced costs by £160 million on a £1.2 billion turnover in five years.
- BP Chemicals' net saving over a two year period was £120 million.
- Sony UK reduced process defects in a factory by 98.5 per cent to achieve productivity and quality levels as high as the home plants in Japan.

No matter what benefits are highlighted, objections will always be raised and need to be overcome if quality is to be sold to the top team. These often centre around beliefs rather than concrete facts, and may also be unsupported. Four common ones have been identified[47]:

1 Quality goals may interfere with distribution schedules and/or budget objectives in the short term.
2 There is a trade-off between cost and quality.
3 Matching, not exceeding, competitors' quality is the goal.
4 Inferiority of home-produced products and services.

The first area is 'short-termism', and is particularly difficult for operational or production managers who tend to be measured by cost and quantity objectives as well as quality. For example, the plant has to meet its immediate objectives, but the end-users may receive a below-standard product, the servicing people have to deal with complaints and senior management have to deal with the results of all of this. Therefore it is in the latter's interests to see that quality goals are not undermined and that those at a senior level with special responsibility for quality are not overridden by those with product and budgetary responsibilities. They must ensure that a balanced approach is taken at all times.

The second area of trade-off can usually be tackled by the 'cost of quality' approach and the longer-term cost-effectiveness of prevention rather than of correction. These have already been outlined in a previous section.

Thirdly, those who believe that money spent on making quality better than that of the competition is wasted are also short-sighted. It is the basis of differentiation, since today's extras become tomorrow's norm as customers compare offerings or demand better standards.

Finally, a distrust or lack of confidence in the home product or service has to be banished through positive thinking and self-image and the publicizing of results. Senior management need to believe in their ability to correctly handle the unexpected events which might affect quality but which, in the end, may be offered as an excuse.

There is also another hurdle to be overcome. Quality-focused companies have to change their management style and practice. In the short term, the emphasis on surfacing problems, delegation, openness and consultation may seem to generate more rather than fewer difficulties for management in the short term. However, in the longer term there are benefits in motivation and commitment and through working 'smarter, not harder'. Selling the benefits and overcoming objections needs to be directed to one purpose: convincing managers that these changes will ensure that they meet their own targets and perform effectively.

2.17 OWN BRAND OR BUY IN QUALITY?

One of the difficulties facing the board and the top team is knowing the degree of outside help needed; whether to adopt a particular approach to get started or 'learn as we go along'. One fundamental problem is the attitudes and values towards quality of those who are in the organization. In an article by the author[48], a tripartite typology of managers' attitudes was outlined, based on experiences of teaching and discussing the subject with groups of managers. Each of the groups – atheists, agnostics and apostles (Fig. 2.4) – had its own concerns, needs and learning requirements.

Atheists were that often very articulate group who stated that the quality philosophy was clearly the figment of someone's imagination. This view had been adopted from a strong *a priori* position and a dislike of the hype:

- It's commonsense management
- Old wine in new bottles

or had evolved from bitter disappointment:

- We put 48 000 people through a one-day seminar and there was nothing more
- A board director was given responsibility, but nothing happened.

The concerns of this group were the setting up of quality programmes, sustaining them, possible detrimental side-effects and value for money. Their needs were to have dispelled the negative emotions, returning to a more neutral stance where they would at least listen and review their position. They learned by discussing the success stories of others and analysing why their organization's initiatives had failed.

One way to manage this was to take as the starting point a strategic view of quality. This stressed competitive advantage, the 'price of entry to markets' and the link to profitability for both cost reduction and increase in market share. This provided an opportunity for managers to stand outside their immediate organizational experience. Broader environmental perspectives such as supply chain management or alliances helped them to see the wider implications of managing for quality. The key aim in this situation was to engender *receptivity*.

The *agnostics* thought that there might just be something in TQM and could be convinced provided the arguments were strong enough. They needed definitions, knowledge inputs, applications, frameworks, best practice and answers to their many questions (Fig. 2.4). The route taken

Quality orientation	Concerns	Needs	Action	Goal
Atheists	● Does TQM exist? ● Start-up difficulty ● Bad side-effects ● Sustaining quality ● Value for money ● 'Old wine in new bottles' ● Temporary fad	● Defuse emotion ● Counteract negatives ● Analytical knowledge (for failure analysis) ● Exposure to successes	● Explore environment perspective ● Take a strategic view ● Use case studies ● Show cost/ benefits of quality	● Receptivity
Agnostics	● What is TQM? ● Is TQM quality circles, BS5750, QA, etc.? ● Where is it applied? ● What are the elements? ● How long does it take? ● What degree of involvement is necessary?	● Definitions ● Illustrations ● Frameworks ● Success stories	● Explore perceptions ● Take empathic departure point ● Provide model to review own situation	● Reassurance
Apostles	● Others not enthusiasts ● Too much emphasis on measurement and control ● Education and problem solving should make supervision redundant	● Systematic appraisal ● Reflection when progressing down TQM route ● Yardsticks to measure progress/ effects of TQM ● Counterbalances	● Offer awareness of tools ● Use new perspectives	● Reasoned argument

FIGURE 2.4   A typology of quality orientations

Source: F.A. Clark, 'Quality, the New Holy Grail: Reflections of a Management Developer'. Reproduced with permission from the *Journal of Managerial Psychology*, Spotlight Centrepiece, pp i–iii. Vol. 7, No. 6, 1992

here was to explore managers' attitudes about customer satisfaction and customer care and to use a video on service with which they could empathize as managers. This triggered questions about empowerment, discretion, management style and risk management within their own organization. For this group to embark on a quality programme or feel competent in persuading others of the case for it, what was needed was *reassurance*.

Finally, there were the *apostles* or missionaries. They generated great enthusiasm, having been converted to quality as a way of life. If obstacles existed or doubts were raised by unbelievers, they dissolved in the face of strong belief and commitment to their ideal. It almost appeared that they had been led down a track without fully appreciating the dilemmas and wider implications of TQM or links to business practice. The type of comments made were:

● 'It's all about attitudes, a new culture'
● 'You don't need to link it to appraisal and reward'.

This group thought that TQM was self-sustaining. They did not see that TQM needed to be consciously embedded in all parts of the organizational fabric: mission, structure, systems, performance management appraisal and reward. Commitment would ensure success as everyone would be working to a common goal. Their concerns were that there was too much emphasis on individual measurement and control, which were unnecessary in a quality management environment. Often these apostles were only a year or so into the implementation of quality. This group needed a more systematic approach, checklists or a means of self-questioning and some yardsticks to measure progress. These could be a useful counterbalance to runaway enthusiasm which might not recognize the seriousness of some of the issues. Apostles needed to be more aware of pragmatic tools such as competitive benchmarking, best practice and cost–benefit analysis. To have a balanced dialogue with anyone, or understand the difficulties of those in the other two groups, they needed a reasoned *argument*.

From this, one might conclude that buying in a package might give reassurance to the agnostics (as it would be accompanied by a list of 'big name' clients), but it would upset the atheists, as the basic propositions would not have been challenged. Developing one's own organizational approach would please the apostles, since their strong faith in the philosophical and attitudinal aspects would carry them through; however, such uncertainties would cause the agnostics to waiver because of a lack of any framework and the atheists to scorn because of a lack of any empirical evidence. The atheists, if they were to be converted, would probably be happier to 'cherry pick' and make comparisons between fact and fiction. Again, this would be unnerving for the agnostics, as there would be no stable point of reference, and irritating for the apostles, who would see it as detracting from a holistic view. The develop or buy-in decision will depend on the prevalence of different types of attitudes. It is therefore important to know to which camp the decision makers belong.

2.18 CONCLUSION

This chapter has provided an overview of some of the strategic thinking which is necessary before embarking on a quality programme. Without a strategic view, culture change, quality audits, benchmarking and all the tools and techniques lose their cutting edge, as there is no clear focus for the quality improvements. Unless quality initiatives are considered within a strategic and multidisciplinary context they will founder, as there will be no funds from senior management to buy the ship, no resources to keep it afloat, and no anchor to stop it drifting off course. Nor will there be commitment to keep it going if the organization runs into troubled waters. However, strategy needs to be underpinned by structure, and this is addressed in the next chapter.

ACTION QUESTIONS

- Has your organization identified the dimensions of quality which are important to its customers?
- How closely has quality been linked to the overall strategy? Are people clear about what a quality programme is expected to deliver?
- What roles and specific actions have the board and the top team undertaken to underwrite the success of an actual or possible quality initiative?

REFERENCES

1 Niven, D. (1993): 'When Times Get Tough, What happens to TQM?' *Harvard Business Review*, May–June, pp. 20–34.

2 Porter, M. (1980): *Competitive Advantage*, The Free Press, New York, USA.

3 Buzzell, R.D. and Gale, B.T. (1987): *The PIMS Principles: Linking Strategy to Performance*, The Free Press, New York, USA.

4 Ross, J.E. and Shetty, Y.K. (1985): 'Making Quality a Fundamental Part of Strategy', *Long Range Planning*, **18**(1), pp. 53–8.

5 Evans, D. (1993): 'User Sues DEC Supplier Over £1.5 million Stores System', *Computer Weekly*, 18 February.

6 Vowler, J. (1993): ed. *Software News*: 'Suppliers Price Hikes Slammed by Major User', *Computer Weekly*, 18 February.

7 Stevens, G.C. (1990): 'Successful Supply Chain Management', *Management Decision*, **28**(8), pp. 25–30.

8 Williams, I. and Birchall, D.W. (1993): 'Does Strategic Partnering in the Supply Chain Have a Future?', *Logistics Technology International*, November, pp. 79–81.

9 Tang, V. and Collar, E. (1992): 'IBMAS/400 New Product Launch Process Ensures Satisfaction', *Long Range Planning*, **25**(1), pp. 22–7.

10 Hodgson, A. (1987): 'Deming's Never Ending Road to Quality', *Personnel Management*, July, pp. 40–4.

11 Walker, R. (1992): 'Rank Xerox Management Revolution', *Long Range Planning*, **25**(1), pp. 9–21.

12 Shetty, Y.K. (1991): 'Competing Through Quality', Sundridge Park, *Management Review*, Spring 1991, **4**(3), pp. 16–21.

13 Kanter, R.M. (1989): *When Giants Learn to Dance*, Simon and Schuster, New York, USA.

14 Garvin, D.A. (1988): *Managing Quality: The Strategic and Competitive Edge*, The Free Press, New York, USA.

15 Garvin, D.A. (1988), op. cit.

16 Garvin, D.A. (1988), op. cit.

17 Garvin, D.A. (1988), op. cit.

18 Parasuraman, A., Zeithaml, V.A. and Berry, L.L. (1985): 'A Conceptual Model of Service Quality and its Implications for Future Research', *Journal of Marketing*, Fall, pp. 41–50.

19 Gronroos, C. (1984): *Strategic Management and Marketing in the*

Service Sector, Chartwell Bratt, Bromley, Kent, UK.

20 Clark, F.A. (1992): 'Quality and Service in the Public Sector', *Public Finance and Accountancy*, 23 October, pp. 23–35.

21 Luchs, B. (1990): 'Quality as a Strategic Weapon: Measuring Relative Quality, Value and Market Differentiation', *European Business Journal*, **2**(4), pp. 34–47.

22 Porter, M. (1980), op. cit.

23 Luchs, B. (1990), op. cit.

24 Shycon, H.N. (1992): 'Improved Customer Service: Measuring the Payoff', *Journal of Business Strategy*, January/February, pp. 13–17.

25 Department of Trade and Industry (1993): *Managing in the '90s. The Competitive Response*, DTI, London, UK.

26 Garvin, D.A. (1988), op. cit.

27 Hughes, D. (1991): 'Motorola Nears Quality Benchmark After Twelve Year Evolutionary Effort', *Aviation Week and Space Technology*, 9 December, pp. 64–5.

28 Chase, R.B. and Garvin, D.A. (1989): 'The Service Factory', *Harvard Business Review*, July/August.

29 Parasuraman, A., Zeithaml, V.A. and Berry, L.L. (1985), op. cit.

30 Clark, F.A. (1992): 'Public Awareness', *Total Quality Management Magazine*, December, pp. 373–8.

31 Zeithaml, V.A., Parasuraman, A. and Berry, L.L. (1990): *Delivering Quality Services*, The Free Press, New York, USA.

32 Shetty, Y.K. (1991), op. cit.

33 Gale B.T. and Klavans, R. (1985): 'Formulating a Quality Improvement Strategy', *Journal of Business Strategy*, **5**(3), Winter, pp. 21–32.

34 Arter, D.R. (1989): *Quality Audits for Improved Performance*, ASQ Quality Press, Wisconsin, USA.

35 Arter, D.R. (1989), op. cit.

36 Garvin, D.A. (1988), op. cit.

37 Niven, D. (1993), op. cit.

38 Niven, D. (1993), op. cit.

39 Ross, J.E. and Shetty, Y.K. (1985), op. cit.

40 Carlzon, J. (1987): *Moments of Truth*, Ballinger Publishing Company, Wisconsin, USA.

41 Shetty, Y.K. (1991), op. cit.

42 Davis, E. (1990): 'High Quality, Positioning, and the Success of

Reputable Products', *Business Strategy Review*, Summer, **1**(2), pp. 61–75.

43 Pearce, J.A. and Zahra, S.A. (1992): 'Board Composition from a Strategic Contingency Perspective', *Journal of Management Studies*, **29**(4), July, pp. 411–38.

44 Clutterbuck, D. and Waine, P. (1993): *The Independent Board Director*, McGraw-Hill, Maidenhead, UK.

45 Pickard, J. (1993): 'When Employees Answer Back', *Personnel Management Plus*, September, pp. 20–1.

46 Drucker, P.F. (1992): *Managing for the Future*, Truman Talley Books, New York, USA.

47 Reddy, J. (1980): 'Incorporating Quality in Competitive Strategies', *Sloan Management Review*, Spring, pp. 53–60.

48 Clark, F.A. (1992) 'Quality, the New Holy Grail? Reflections of a Management Developer', *Journal of Managerial Psychology*, **7**(6), Spotlight Centrepiece, pp.i–iii.

Structures for delivering quality

3.1 INTRODUCTION

One important function of a leader is to ensure that the appropriate organization structures are in place to deliver quality. A fundamental belief underpinning the quality philosophy is that unnecessary or restrictive forms of organization need to be removed to give people the flexibility and creativity they need to allow for continuous improvement. Nevertheless, some formal organization is necessary for quality programmes to have direction and impetus.

Analysing a sample of 106 visitors to a quality exhibition at the National Exhibition Centre, the author found 17 job titles containing the word 'quality' and, within them, an implication of an approximate hierarchy, as follows:

- Group Quality Director
- Director of Quality, UK
- Quality Support Manager
- Quality Coordinator
- Quality Assurance Manager
- Quality Facilitator

There are obviously a number of combinations and permutations found across all sectors as organizations strive to find a structure of management that will meet their specific needs.

The experience of Florida Power and Light, however, warns against an over-elaborate hierarchy which can be costly and stifling. Former winner of the Malcolm Baldridge Award, FPL, subsequently dismantled most of its quality hierarchy since it was adding nothing to the company's goal of service quality.

Whatever configuration an organization adopts for quality, it is necessary to examine the general structural changes which are occurring and which can impact on the type of quality organization adopted. The next section therefore examines the emerging forms of organization, what they are supposed to deliver and their managerial implications for quality.

3.2 CURRENT AND NEW WAYS OF ORGANIZING

It is not intended here to deliver a detailed analysis of new forms of organization, as they have been summarized elsewhere[1]. However, there are a number of common themes which are recognizable almost everywhere. Organizations are becoming decentralized, removing in droves corporate IT departments, accountants, human resources specialists and other support roles without direct links to line management. The moving of BP and Shell's IT staff roles to subcontractors is a good example of this.

With decentralization comes autonomy, profit and cost responsibility handled at a business or local unit level. Federalism is now the watchword, with centres of excellence to be accessed and shared by all. These are located not in some corporate, central headquarters, but within one of the constituent parts of the organization and to which funds will be attracted. The call is thus to dual citizenship and the sharing of information and resources through informal networks to carry out the work.

Flatter organizations are now appearing everywhere. Those such as BP and British Gas, which had up to 13 layers, are now operating with five or six. Middle management has been virtually rooted out, as more junior staff are expected to manage themselves in relation to clearly specified objectives and systems while at the same time showing more discretion in their work against predefined standards and values.

Many enterprises are evolving towards the 'core-periphery' type of structure with a small core of professionals, contract workers and hired helps on demand. Whole functions are now being outsourced. BP exploration has given contracts to outside organizations to handle its IT and accounting functions, and it is now common practice to outsource areas such as security and catering. This whole area is discussed in more detail in Chapter 9.

3.3 WHAT THESE ORGANIZATIONAL FORMS ARE EXPECTED TO DELIVER

First and foremost, these changes are designed to ensure that organizations are 'closer to the customer'. Fewer layers in the hierarchy mean that management is not so remote from what is happening in the field. Lengthy waits for operational decisions can be reduced. Approvals to modify customer policy, give reassurance on delivery or to rectify errors can occur within a timespan which does not conflict with customer expectations. The resulting empowerment means that problem solving is faster and that the relevant knowledge is concentrated where it matters most.

A good example is cited[2] by the former president of Scandinavian Airline System (SAS). Annually, some 10 million customers were served by around five employees each and the contact time was on average 15 seconds. Therefore SAS had 50 million 'moments of truth' in which to impress those customers.

> If they have to go up the organizational chain of command for a decision on an individual problem, then those 15 golden seconds will elapse without a response and we will have lost an opportunity to earn a loyal customer.

Greater autonomy and decentralization are designed to deliver responsiveness and flexibility. Local market needs are said to be better served through this policy, as parts of the organization are not hampered, in delivering their services, by corporate procedures, controls and finances. A sense of team spirit is easier to generate because of perceived greater control, and this in turn leads to a sense of commitment to the cause. It is worth trying to do a good job because there is more of a direct link between effort and performance.

3.4 MANAGERIAL IMPLICATIONS FOR QUALITY

The new structures and anticipated deliverables are not without their problems, especially if an organization is shifting from an old to a new form. Take the 'core-periphery' form, for example. If all the training and development is focused on the core, what sort of commitment will there be to the organization and to delivering quality from the contractual fringe and the hired helps? Why should they feel bound to turn down work from competitors and why should they stay around to see a project through if they are only on one week's notice, if that is what the organization has given them? Engineering companies often run on these arrangements, not wanting to commit themselves beyond the end of a working week. The result is that the permanent staff are always ready to 'blame' the contractor (who may have been expressly hired to 'sort out' a complicated muddle created by permanent staff in the first place and compounded by a succession of previous contract staff). The irony of the situation is that the very person who has probably come nearest to the root of the problem and who could provide continuity has long since left.

The practice of outsourcing the work of whole departments raises similar questions, but on a larger scale (see again Chapter 9). Will those undertaking the work put their best staff onto the contract to win it and then phase themselves out with more junior or less experienced staff? Will the client become a training ground for new staff? How secure will the information be, and could it inadvertently be passed on to third parties?

On the question of training, while it may seem superficially cost-effective to train only those at the core whom the organization believes will stay, in the longer term it can only be self-defeating if the skill and knowledge differential between 'insider' and 'outsider' increases. The quality chain is only as strong as its weakest link.

With different categories of organizational membership, managing the boundaries is likely to be problematical. There is usually more internal managerial effort required to manage external staff. The latter will always have their own purpose and mission, resulting in priorities which may not be those of their contract employer.

Another implication of the flatter structure is that managers can no longer distance themselves from their staff, hiding behind status or seniority. As such, their behaviour (or lack of it) is more exposed and subject to closer scrutiny and questioning. However, interpreted in this way, it is a negative approach to take. More positively, the implications for the management of quality are that managers are more in touch with the thoughts and feelings of their staff and their dealings with customers (internal and external). In addition, the authority and responsibility for dealing with customers is located closer to the interface at which service decisions need to be made.

In the absence of formal structures, informal networks will spring up which cut across the functions and divisions of an organization to enable the speedy execution of work. To merely speak of networks, however, belies their purpose and complexity. A useful distinction has been made[3] between three types of network:

- *advice* (key players on whom others depend to provide technical information and solve problems)
- *trust* (share delicate political information; back each other in a crisis; moan about the poor state of affairs)
- *communications* (talk about work-related matters regularly).

The researchers showed that mapping advice networks can uncover the source of political conflicts and failure to achieve strategic objectives because these show the key influences. Trust networks show up non-routine problems and performance of temporary teams and communications networks can identify gaps in information flow.

Five common configurations exist which managers can explore to see whether they are working to enhance or hinder their goals:

1 *Imploded relationships* (employees talk only with those inside the group; only those who are senior have contacts outside and they may 'hoard' these, not introducing them to junior staff).
2 *Irregular communications* (employees communicate with those outside the group and not among themselves).
3 *Fragile structures* (employees communicate among themselves and with one other division).
4 *Holes* (places where you would expect to find relationship ties but do not).
5 *'Bow ties'* (many players depend on a single employee but not on each other. He or she is the centre knot of the bow tie).

Reducing complexity at a formal level means getting to grips with it at an informal level. Managers need to understand these relationships better if they want to manage a wider span of staff. With a reduced hierarchy, there is less direct supervision and more of a need for individuals to learn (since that is what continuous improvement means in practical terms). Problem solving, improving a product or service or redesigning a process all require an ability to learn. Learning can be described as a change in behaviour or attitude due to experience. Hence the focus has shifted to the learning organization, described[4] as an environment:

where people continually expand their capacities to create the results they truly desire, where new and expansive patterns of thinking are nurtured, where collective aspirations are set free and where people are continually learning how to learn together.

This would be done through five component technologies: systems thinking, personal mastery, mental models, shared vision and team learning. However, it has been pointed out[5] that the actual details of how this works in practice are left unclear.

Unless the behaviour modification takes place, the learning offers only the potential for improvement, not the reality. Organizations cited as exemplifying this orientation are Honda, Corning and General Electric. The five main activities are:

1 *Systematic problem solving* (Xerox's problem-solving process).
2 *Experimentation* (Corning's search for new ways of making better grades of glass).
3 *Learning from experience* (Boeing commissioned a task force to examine the development process of the problem 737 and 747 aeroplanes. This was to tease out the lessons and apply them to the development of a new model).
4 *Learning from others* (benchmarking with other suppliers and customers).
5 *Transferring knowledge* (education and training, rotation of personnel, transfer of expertise into different environments).

Measuring the learning is perhaps the most difficult thing to do. Notions such as the experience curve which focus only on the reduction in cost or price do not take into account other competitive variables such as quality. An alternative is to conduct a learning audit covering different types of improvement:

● *cognitive* (the absorption of new ideas)
● *behavioural* (the alteration of behaviour)
● *performance improvement* (how the output has changed).

The balance of these will vary according to the organization and change programme.

Another concept which has gained ground is business process management (Chapter 9). A major obstacle to performance has been the focus on functions within organizations (known as the 'silo' effect). This has had detrimental effects on the horizontal links to manage the 'white spaces' within the vertically conceived reporting lines. However, the horizontal management of customer-oriented processes is vital to the delivery of goods and services so that they present a seamless transition of activity to meet customer needs.

3.5 INTERNAL STRUCTURES AND SYSTEMS FOR QUALITY

There is no agreed 'best way' to organize for quality except that it needs to be ingrained in the structure of the organization, not imposed on it. While quality is the responsibility of everyone, effort needs to be harnessed and focused in a variety of ways. A number of themes recur in the approaches taken.

The efforts put into quality need to be harnessed and directed towards the organization's goals and strategies. Typically, the top management team will set up a quality council to see that this end is achieved. It may approve company-wide schemes, allocate funds and resources and ensure that the appropriate benchmarking exercises are carried out. The council or steering committee typically has a remit to establish:

- awareness of the competitive challenge throughout the organization
- a vision for the future and leadership for the change effort
- a process to encourage innovation and develop appropriate technology
- a process for broad employee involvement
- a proper organizational structure for the effort and a plan to guide it
- total quality improvement as a way of life in the organization.

The Royal Mail Strategy Steering Group shows the importance of integrating quality into the system, and is discussed later in the chapter.

There may also be a small centre of excellence, with a few central staff headed by a quality director or manager whose role is to advise, support and act as a central information point for best practice coming from within and outside the organization. As a result of this privileged position, information can be redirected to encourage other parties to share ideas and concerns with each other. This happens, for example, at Texaco, with the director of quality reporting in to finance.

Line managers' involvement is also a common theme. They need to give their support in training, encouraging and delivering quality. Typically, volunteers may be called in to develop the necessary training and facilitation skills to start the process. However, removing them totally from their line management roles can cause problems for the individual and the organization. For a line manager, there are potential problems of skills and knowledge becoming out-of-date, resulting in loss of credibility when the threads of an old job have to be picked up later. For the organization, there are problems in creating the job to move people back into the line, as BT and others have found.

Various divisional or business unit teams may also be set up, composed of line managers, some with special responsibility for bringing in new ideas or providing advice in addition to their normal duties. They may help to formulate the quality guidelines and standards. They may also encourage or approve projects which may be cross-divisional and require quality improvement teams, or support the introduction of quality circles (based around the natural work unit). An example of how one business, Royal Mail, organized itself for quality is given below.

Within Royal Mail, there are a number of strategy steering groups. These are a cross-functional focal point for the development of strategies which may be implemented throughout the organization. The groups are led by a member of the Royal Mail Executive Committee. This person is also a line manager for one of the divisions and may call upon other senior people from a range of strategy groups, which provides a wider perspective than if a group were made up solely of functional specialists. These groups define transformational programmes and determine those performance measurements which will help monitor their implementation. They are the champions of these initiatives in providing resources and support.

One of these groups is the Total Quality Strategy Steering Group. It provides strategic direction in many areas: 'customer first' programme, monitoring continuous improvement, benchmarking, participation in quality awards and developing tools and techniques to maintain the total quality initiative. The group relates to other parts of the organization, as indicated in Fig. 3.1.

The Total Quality Strategy Steering Group is supported by a number of 'focus groups', each led by a member of the quality department based at the strategic headquarters. The focus groups support the Total Quality Strategy Steering Group by assisting in the formulation of strategic plans for the Royal Mail Executive Committee and in recommending modifications or

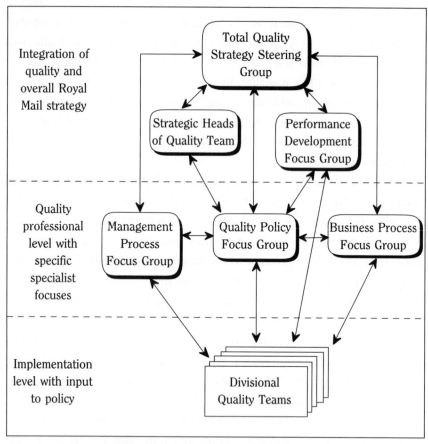

Integration of quality and overall Royal Mail strategy

Quality professional level with specific specialist focuses

Implementation level with input to policy

FIGURE 3.1 Royal Mail's total quality strategy steering group and focus groups

Source: Reproduced with permission from Royal Mail (1995)

changes to any existing programmes. Once they are agreed, the focus group helps to design and support the implementation of these initiatives.

There are three quality focus groups, each with its own remit to support the Total Quality Strategy Steering Group. Their roles are as follows:

- *quality policy* (developing policy based on strategic direction);
- *business process* (improving performance by targeting key business processes and using models, tools and techniques);
- *management process* (evolving policies to help management integrate different facets of the quality strategy, for example, planning, benchmarking and business excellence reviews).

In the divisions, there are two main supporting parts of the quality structure. The first is the quality improvement team (QIP). These groups of staff meet regularly to make work-related improvements in areas of importance to them. Participation is voluntary and the groups meet mainly during working hours. The team selects its leader and may also have a trained facilitator to provide specialist knowledge. The group, if possible, should be able to implement any changes and, if necessary, call upon the support of its manager or the quality guidance group (QGG). This is the second element in the divisional quality structure. It coordinates, encourages and supports effective employee involvement by providing advice to the QIPs, management and unions. Membership is drawn from different roles and functions across the divisions. The group helps teams to select suitable projects from ideas put forward by all employees and provides help both at the start and also by communicating their achievements.

The important thing to note about these structures is that they are not static, but evolve with the needs of the business and, indeed, the needs of the quality programme itself. For example, Royal Mail has annually reviewed the role and contribution of the quality support managers to ensure that they are still relevant, and made the reporting arrangements and meetings part of the day-to-day running of the organization.

With American Express (Travel Related Services) the 'reach' of the quality staff is worldwide. Quality assurance staff are present in every country in which a card operations centre exists. Similarly, Johnson and Johnson operates a Quality Institute, from which senior staff work internationally in support of locally-based quality staff.

The importance that organizations attach to quality is seen in the level of involvement of the board. At one division of Westland Helicopters any quality project is carried out under the sponsorship of a board member. Thus resources can be put behind the project, and if it is delayed, there will be peer pressure at the highest level. Similarly, the title accorded to quality professionals is also an indication of the importance attached to quality. For example, at Amex, the CEO is also the director of quality.

At Rank Xerox, a corporate quality office was established and headed by a vice-president, underscoring the commitment of top management to the role. Again, at the core of British Airways' continuous improvement process is a corporate quality board. This has been responsible for developing an internal self-assessment scheme based on the Malcolm Baldridge and European Quality Award criteria. It has also established a process for organizing cross-functional and cross-hierarchical improvement activities. It is creating an infrastructure for the roll-out of corporate-wide continuous improvement groups. Some 70 facilitators are being trained to teach the continuous improvement groups themselves and to instruct team leaders to head them at all levels.

3.6 QUALITY CIRCLES REVISITED

One key component of the organizational structure for quality is the use of quality circles. These are typically a small day-to-day work group, say, eight people, who have had some training in problem-solving techniques. They meet regularly to identify, analyse, tackle problems and suggest improvements within their areas of responsibility. Originally started in Japan in the 1960s, they have been used by several organizations, such as Honeywell, and 3M, and cover many sectors, such as education, manufacturing and financial services. A particularly strong exponent of the technique in this country is Sony.

However, quality circles have had mixed success as a management tool. Often they have a honeymoon period and then fade away after two years. A recent survey[7] of both the literature and an empirical study in a manufacturing environment yielded a list of factors which needed careful consideration:

- top management commitment
- training of participants
- middle management commitment
- voluntary participation
- clear objectives
- adherence to the quality circle process
- feedback to quality circles
- rewards offered for participation.

These are all areas where sound leadership training pays off.

Companies such as Rank Xerox and British Airways not only provide training, but also issue staff with customized pocket books for reference. These typically contain information about the steps in the problem-solving process, specific techniques such as cause–effect diagrams, Pareto analysis, data gathering techniques and recording, simple statistical process control charts, project management and brainstorming. The quality circles process is itself important and should be part of a wider programme of improvement with a steering committee. The problems selected are those over which individuals have some control and to which they can apply first-hand knowledge. The group should also have access to an external facilitator should the need arise. Rewards should also be considered. However, as with suggestion schemes, the intrinsic rewards such as recognition, personal development and skill enhancement need to be emphasized rather than monetary rewards, as these soon lose their motivating power.

The author recently observed at first hand a service organization which attempted to introduce quality circles. First, top management had no mission and values statement nor a quality policy. There was no structure for quality into which the suggestions could be integrated. Participants were not trained (as in the examples given above), but were told that the groups were there to think up improvements and solve problems. This was after a brief introduction by the CEO which was more exhortation than content. The managers themselves were untrained in management, quite apart from not having any background in the quality field (just like their bosses). Membership was not voluntary and the groups felt that they were under the spotlight as guinea pigs. If things worked out well, the process would spread; if not, the damage could be limited. This signalled to them the 'distancing' from the process of senior management who did not really believe that they would succeed. The process was adhered to in a mechanical fashion (rather than developed) and there were no links to other aspects of the organization's need for quality improvement.

3.7 TASK FORCES (OR IMPROVEMENT GROUPS)

While quality circles focus on existing work roles based on permanent groupings around areas of responsibility within their own control, not all problems or company initiatives can be so neatly parcelled. Other kinds of improvement can only come from those in the horizontal and vertical chains providing a broader perspective and a willingness to alter their part for the greater good. These task forces, corrective action teams, or improvement groups are temporary in nature. They tackle important processes or organization-wide problems which cut across traditional commercial, technical and administrative boundaries, and the problems they solve are generated as part of a wider strategy for policy or a company improvement plan.

However, because these groups are tackling long-term problems they may begin to take on an aura of autonomy and power, and this has to be managed. First, these groups may expand their horizons and influence, giving them access to information and a hearing at the highest levels where they would not normally be consulted. This generates a feeling of exclusivity which can defeat their purpose if they are not properly managed. Once given a taste of this freedom, they may be difficult to disband, since the group may wish to prolong its identity well beyond the required life of the project. While developing individuals, this can also be detrimental to them, as they may become out of touch with their normal role and become impatient to be promoted out of it. It may be difficult for the organization to find them a suitable position once the project has ended. Therefore the group needs clear objectives, a decision as to whether members will be seconded full- or part-time from their jobs, and a series of review meetings and deadlines so that they are accountable and know that their involvement both as individuals and as group members may be altered or terminated.

As with quality circles, the group should have clear terms of reference and scope of responsibilities defined for it and then revisit them after a month or so to see whether the project and the team as conceived are feasible. Any team needs time to warm up and adjust before plunging straight into task objectives. Indeed, if this is not done the task is liable to fail because of a poor process for organizing work and handling conflict.

3.8 INTERNAL CUSTOMER GROUPINGS

Part of the skill for organizing for quality is to be sure who one's internal customers are, at an individual, group or functional level. For example, the R&D function is a supplier to marketing. On the other hand, too inflexible an application of quality management concepts may alienate functions from each other. For example, 'right first time' will not translate so easily to an innovative and non-repetitive environment, and breaking down the output of R&D from the customer's viewpoint may be more problematical. Moreover, the customers may not readily realize the marketing potential of the information with which they are readily provided. Another example may be measuring the cost of quality. Resources wasted on output which is not used are difficult to measure, since the resources could have been exploited for a business opportunity of unknown value.

Similarly, the personnel function has for its customers senior line managers. They indicate their key operational objectives which are set in a matrix against the services provided by (or derived from) the personnel function. For each cell managers are asked whether the personnel contribution has helped, hindered or had no impact on the achievement of the service. There should also be a corporate input into the desired services, for example corporate change programmes or culture assessment.

3.9 Customer care units

Customer care is so important that many organizations have a head of customer services. Scanning advertisements for such posts, it appears that a key aspect of the job is to strengthen relations with other functions to ensure that an integrated service is delivered. The complexity of this role is illustrated by one advertisement which required, among other things, the following roles and activities:

- contribution to strategic policy for customer services
- exceeding customer satisfaction targets by providing leadership to the customer services unit
- identify new working practices
- develop a customer services unit plan driving service improvement across the business.

Although customer care is ultimately everyone's responsibility, most organizations have a focal point which customers can contact. Customer care units are part of a wider customer care programme. The latter have, as their aims, the retention of customers; increase of brand loyalty; differentiation of product or service; enhanced reputation; and competitive edge. Often there will be some form of customer charter (as with BT, BR, the water and electricity companies) which advises customers of what standards of service they may expect and what compensation exists if things go wrong. For example, SEEBOARD, the electricity company, guarantees to restore supplies within 24 hours. If this takes longer, they will pay £40 if the customer is domestic and £100 if commercial.

The contribution of a customer care unit is generally expected to be:

- to identify the current level of service
- to show consistency with what is delivered
- to advise those who are managing it
- to know what proportion of contacts are enquiries, queries or complaints
- to understand where the repeat purchases are coming from.

All this information must be fed back in a way which contributes to improving the marketing and quality effort in the organization.

The customer care unit may come into contact with the customer in a number of different ways: primary (face to face, or voice to voice); secondary (advertising, letters); and third party. In the first two cases there is direct control over the interaction and the organization can review its policy and service levels. The appropriate organization and management will depend on the time the employee actually spends dealing with the customers, the pressure on the employee for allocated time spent, and peaks and troughs. The measure of the commitment to customer care is the degree of authority and responsibility to take action that is given to staff and the limits of their discretion. Putting employees onto schedules requiring so many calls to be dealt with per hour is contradicting the very reason why people contact customer care units – it is a personal service which cannot be delivered through recordings and standard procedures.

British Telecom improved the way it handled complaints by enabling customers to be referred from one part of the business to another using its Customer Service System (CSS) database. The customer contact handling system (which is part of the CSS) enables customer reception people to log customer contacts. Study groups from across business divisions have reviewed procedures and focused on areas for improvement. One of the outcomes of this is a customer appeals procedure. This offers an alternative to contacting Oftel (the industry watchdog) if customers are not satisfied with the way that complaints are handled.

The telephone is the most crucial contact point. Quality-oriented organizations such as Amex have strict requirements that calls are answered within two rings. This implies that some preparatory work has been done to ensure an adequate number of lines for the traffic, that they are channelled to the correct organizational points and that the staff are there to answer. Credit card companies such as NatWest have a 24-hour-a-day, seven-days-a-week service to cover all eventualities. Petrol suppliers, too, have extended their coverage to help forecourt managers in the event of supplies not being delivered in time.

Consideration needs to be given to the name of the customer care unit and its role. Dissatisfied customers can be difficult, but they provide the opportunity to eliminate sources of error in the service and may also be a valuable source of ideas for improvement, as the type of comments below illustrate:

- If only you could do this we would not have a problem
- I've seen things done this way elsewhere; why can't you do it?

Milliken, the 1993 winner of the European Quality Award, follows up every delivery with two questions: Was everything all right? Can we do anything better? Moreover, calling a unit a complaints unit or publicizing it as such can cause problems, implying that things are bound to go wrong. A manager in a benefits office said to me that the walls were covered in posters telling people how to complain. So, while they were sitting waiting to be seen, what better to do than assume they ought to find a problem and now would be the chance to do something about it! Philips Electronics service division used to have their own vans with a special livery, saying: 'Always available, rarely required'. It was a clever way of advertising their service if things had gone wrong for their customers, without implying that they were likely to.

There will always be complaints, justified or unjustified. However, there should always be a clear procedure for logging them, dealing with them and signing them off as having been completed to the satisfaction of the customer or client. The process needs to be systematized through forms or a screen-based system, giving all the customer details, the nature of the problem, the action to be taken and the recording of customer comments. The date and those involved in the process should also be recorded. British Telecom has a special service to help its staff deal with customer complaints. The helpline (with a number known only to them) is available to resolve problems which have been channelled through the standard public numbers (for example, 151 for customer repairs) but are still outstanding.

There should also be a manager in charge, of suitable status to be able to ensure that appropriate individuals, can, if necessary, be brought together to solve the problem. The manager may also need a champion at director level if there are major policy or procedural issues involved. A well-respected and major Swiss bank once lost a customer, itself a national European bank, through an uncharacteristic poor settlement procedure on one of its investment transactions. It believed this to be so damaging to its reputation that it set up a special unit in its back office to log every incident. The completed forms then had to be signed off by the manager of the unit and the board-level director so that, apart from ensuring a satisfactory response, other members of the bank could be aware of what had happened if they were doing business with the customer. This at least conveyed a clear intent not to repeat the mistake and showed that a board-level interest was being taken in delivering the service and in mending any fences. Thus leadership was demonstrated by example and not by exhortation alone.

By systematically collecting, analysing and disseminating information, useful ideas may be gleaned about the patterns in the timing or nature of the complaints, whether they were person- or product-centred and their seriousness. In one Philips factory, part of it was sectioned off to take complaints about televisions and their repair. That way, there was a direct line of access from the person responsible for customers to the production line and store, so that expert technical or functional help could be made available quickly when problems arose.

The key reasons for making customer care a priority should never be forgotten:

- It is easier to increase market share by doing business with existing customers than with new ones.
- It costs five times as much to convert a new customer as it does to hold on to a new one.
- Losing customers means that they will probably tell another ten people of their experience.
- Lost opportunities cannot be quantified, as those hearing about poor service will pass it on, probably with embellishment.
- Opportunities for cross-selling are available and already carry credibility.

Customer care units have a vital part to play in linking their structure and systems to other parts of the business and the monitoring and analysis of customer expectations. These can be focused on different things[8]:

- *adequate service* (the standard that customers are willing to accept);
- *desired service* (what customers want);
- *predicted service* (the level of service they believe likely to occur).

Each has its own antecedents or factors which, it is suggested, influence it. These are areas which can be picked up by customer care units and fed into marketing. Taking the adequate service expectations first, these are conditioned by:

- *transitory service intensifiers* (short-term factors which make a customer more sensitive to service, e.g. personal emergency where the expectation of what is adequate service is raised);
- *perceived service alternatives* (customers believe they can obtain it elsewhere);
- *self-perceived service role* (customers' view of how they think they can influence service, as when they believe they are helping the provider to deliver the service);
- *situational factors* (these lower expectations of service as they are deemed to be beyond the role of the service provider (e.g. bad weather)).

Similarly, there are antecedents of desired and predicted service. These are:

- *explicit service promises* (statements, personal and non-personal, made to customers by the organization (for example, advertising, personal selling, contracts));
- *implicit service promises* (service-related cues indicating what the service could be like (for example, price and tangibles));
- *word of mouth* (what people say to each other rather than what the organization says);
- *past experience* (exposure to the firm or to others offering the same service).

Sensitivity to these expectations and whether they are met or not can be a useful marketing tool and requires a positive leadership to extract the maximum information about complaints from the customer care units. They need to be reviewed to see whether they are 'one off' events or the start of a broader trend.

Customer care is exemplified by the Japanese store Daiichi[9]. It sells consumer electronics products which other stores sell but with a difference: 'a powerful information and service system, a feedback loop of customer knowledge'.

First, customers are invited into the store to see a product as a result of the direct mailing and telemarketing programme. When customers purchase a product they receive a three-year warranty instead of the one-year guarantee supplied by the manufacturer; delivery is normally next day. In the third year of warranty, Daiichi offer to send a technician to check over the item before warranty expires and any other appliances, regardless of whether or not they were purchased from Daiichi. On completing the house call, technicians report on the products in the home, their model and age. This is entered into an on-line database which the sales force can access. A salesperson may then write to the individual (knowing, for example, that a particular appliance is nearing the end of its working life) to invite them to visit the store to examine a new model. With this process, some 70 per cent of sales are repeat business. This competitive edge is due to superior knowledge gained from a coordinated customer care process involving the sales, marketing and servicing functions.

One important aspect of the organization structure for customer care units is how they and their systems interface with marketing databases. These have three broad characteristics:

- *sheer scale* (information may be available on millions of households);
- *depth* (thousands of details about each household can be captured, for example, size and purchasing history);
- *targeted usage* (information enables the targeting of small groups of customers).

Clearly, complaints, enquiries and general handling of customers could be linked in to see what sort of customer profile, if any, was emerging. Combinations of frequent shopper databases with demographic lifestyle data could be used to understand more fully customer needs.

3.10 EXTERNAL CUSTOMER GROUPINGS

In devising a structure for quality, many organizations find it useful to form specific groups of customers to generate feedback on quality. Royal Mail has its User Council which helps to monitor performance. Digital have an organization called DECUS (DEC equipment users) which is run by and for non-users with its own spokesperson. The group looks after its own needs and may negotiate, generate requests or provide comments on the type of service it receives. Hewlett Packard, the computer manufacturer, has user groups in various countries. Britain's HP user group has some 600 members and was allowed access to the company's database of customers to conduct a survey at home and abroad. The results were reported in the computer press[10]. The survey showed that the customers were happy with the quality of the computers, but dissatisfied with the level of support given. The cost of assistance with hardware and software problems, poor invoicing and inadequately briefed salespeople were among the key criticisms. The company's rapid expansion both here and abroad had generated a lack of customer care which the company was forced to address.

At a more general level, *Which?* magazine runs its consumer panels, as does the BBC. Where customers do act with a common voice, there are watchdogs to which they can complain. The London International Financial Futures and Options Exchange (LIFFE) has the power to impose penalties. Barclays de Zoete Wedd (BZW) was fined £67,000 in 1993 and penalties were imposed on several employees for completing trading but failing to pass on the best prices obtained by the clients in breach of LIFFE rules. It also found the staff to have acted 'with reckless disregard for the interests of a client'.

3.11 PROCESSING THE FEEDBACK

When information has been collected, nowhere is a leader's example more needed than in being willing to process it. Some of the common reasons why organizations take the trouble to do so are:

● staying in business
● developing new products and services
● gleaning new ideas
● preventing defections.

This last area is a key aspect to mention[11], as defections can have more to do with a service company's profits than scale, market share, unit costs and many other factors usually associated with competitive advantage. By comparing nine industries, it was found that reducing defection rates by 5 per cent boosted profits by between 25 and 85 per cent. By obtaining specific feedback, organizations can root out weaknesses that matter and help themselves to achieve continuous improvement. Organizations are often unaware of the true costs of losing a customer since most ignore anticipated cash flows over a lifetime.

In contrast to conventional market research (which may focus on attitudes or satisfaction, which may be changeable), defecting customers' complaints tend to be concrete and specific[12]. Analysis requires particular, relevant questions. When customers miss ordering one month or stop ordering particular products, an alert organization will telephone to ask why. There may be competitive underpricing or a new alternative allowing the company to change its buying behaviour, warn suppliers or target particular customer segments. It should also indicate which service quality improvements will be the most profitable.

Training for this type of work requires imparting a sense of urgency and importance, communicating the objective of defection analysis, its benefits, and how to gather data, analyse them and pass them on. At this point it is up to senior management to really make use of the results, compare how different branches or businesses are doing with regard to retaining customers and provide a supportive atmosphere to deal with problems. Often the complaints are not about the product or service directly, but about the way in which people have been handled.

Another reason for obtaining feedback is that attributes which customers rate as important are not necessarily those which characterize their views of high-quality firms. For example, a survey of commercial insurance customers[13] showed that the highest ranked attribute was fast and fair payment of claims, which, as a group, insurers tended to do well. However, they were rated much lower in service functions such as effectively handling enquiries (although customers viewed these as less important than claims handling). Nevertheless, these correlated most strongly with customers' rankings of service quality.

There are many different ways of obtaining feedback from customers, as detailed in the following paragraphs. It should be emphasized that one is not necessarily better than another and that these can be used in combination.

Questionnaires can be anonymous or not, depending on the particular purpose of the survey. For example, mailed questionnaires are provided by Royal Mail to regularly survey all their customers on certain key variables as a means of ensuring continuous improvement in quality. Gradually, as certain needs are consistently met, an item may be dropped as it has been incorporated into the service and no longer requires special attention. IBM's share of the world market dropped significantly over the last few years before recovering again. Its worldwide customer satisfaction survey also showed a fall in the results, leading its senior vice-president to initiate a market-driven quality (MDQ) programme to improve satisfaction. IBM's managers, like those of Rank Xerox, are rewarded on the basis of customer ratings, as are those at Royal Mail and other quality-conscious companies. This is where leadership is vital in accepting and using the results.

Post Office Counters branch offices survey customers in their local catchment areas, identifying transactions carried out on an individual basis or a business basis. The questions cover particular areas such as:

- ability of staff to answer questions
- appearance
- welcome
- speed of starting the transaction
- speed of dealing with the transaction.

The above are really to examine the performance of the staff. Also considered are the contextual aspects: privacy; range of services; office appearance; adequacy of open counter positions; availability of the manager; and length of time waiting to be served in the queue. Each item is re-rated for importance and then analysed against classificatory data of the user to see whether the needs of particular groups are being met.

On-site or *location questionnaires* are, for example, those left in a hotel room or in a car immediately after service. They tap reactions to the service in a few minutes, but are less subtle in the questions they ask than their lengthier counterparts. A rating of 'good' for room service does not indicate whether it refers to speed, courtesy, presentation, quality of product and so on.

Telephone surveys naturally provide a more personal touch. Dell Computers offer a 'direct from manufacturer sales and service support, including unlimited telephone problem solving'. They introduced the post of European customer service director when Dell's market share was under severe threat and needed someone to be accountable for service excellence. Customers are now telephoned back on a regular basis to see how satisfied they are with the service received. Complaints and negative comments can then be dealt with promptly.

Direct helplines are also a useful source of information about a customer's needs. Microsoft, the computer software company, is able to access very detailed information. It routes the caller according to specific products used and also if special technical help is needed. Similarly, BT uses its 152 lines to track sales and account queries. These are routed to one of four business customer service centres around London. At one of these, about 80 people deal with up to 4200 calls per day (approximately one every eight minutes), underlining the need for the service.

Advertising campaigns can also be of use. British Telecom has a 'We want your business to ...' campaign which focuses on different customer needs (e.g. mobility – we want your business to stay in touch; access – we want your business to get more from today's communications). In the first week of the campaign some 3000 responses were received. Those who responded to the mobility campaign received charge card details in their pack of literature. For the telemarketing campaign, BT sent out a guide to telemarketing. In this way, it is possible to gauge what is important to customers.

Write-ins are also a way of generating feedback. London Transport (LT) updates its strategy every three years. Before this takes place, LT, via its newsletter *London Direct,* gives notice that there will be consultation booklets and advertising in newspapers and on posters within underground and bus networks to encourage individuals to write in with their ideas on how the system could be improved. For the 1991 campaign, nearly 2000 individuals and groups responded. For the 1994 campaign, particular issues on which LT wanted people to comment were: priorities in spending; improvements in safety, security and accessibility; fares and pricing policy; improvements to buses; enhancement of underground services and problems of congestion; and new lines. This has the effect of anticipating needs and collating negative comments and devoting the time to investigate them.

Distributors or franchisees of products or services are also well placed to provide feedback. They can develop consistent methods of recording information with their suppliers and be well trained in handling queries and problems. A uniformity of recording covering different locations yields valuable information about local patterns of need.

Focus groups are another way to acquire feedback on performance. Being in a group triggers ideas for members and helps people to articulate what may previously have been just vague feelings of satisfaction or dissatisfaction. British Telecom have used focus groups to help build a picture of customers' needs and lifestyles in the UK (for example, when they talk, to whom, what they do and so on).

Shadowing is another useful technique. British Telecom is using this to develop a better understanding of customer needs. Staff are following selected customer representatives for a whole day observing their business and social life. For example, one representative spent time with a company chairman while, by chance, various BT services were being installed. The type and frequency of communication of the chairman was noted, especially the many but short meetings which took place.

Secondment carries this process forward to give an in-depth insight into how customers operate and how they might view an organization's products and services. How it feels to deal with an organization and what problems may occur are important questions for capturing the consequences of poor service and learning from mistakes.

Service staff and engineers are also a good source of feedback. However, since they are usually on a set call rate or schedule, they need to be given time to record and discuss their thoughts.

Delivery and other staff who have casual contacts are also vital. For example, one multinational electronics company was about to purchase a new fleet of delivery trucks. A driver commented that the rear platform would be too high for the loading bays of several customers, so a modification was made, preventing the complaints which would have inevitably followed. Even when the sources of feedback are tapped and analysed there is additional work to do, noting how long it was before the feedback was achieved and, with complaints, the time to resolution.

3.12 TRAINING OF SUPPLIERS

The organization of quality may also extend beyond the immediate boundaries of the organization. The insurance industry uses financial intermediaries who will interface directly with the customer and will therefore represent the company to the client. Quality-conscious organizations such as ICL, Marks and Spencer and Texas Instruments are continually building supportive customer/supplier relationships, while Mars has five principles which describe how it does business. In this context, the mutuality principle is of particular interest to relationships with suppliers. The belief is that 'a mutual benefit is a shared benefit' and that a shared benefit will endure. This enables shared training and product knowledge between supplier and distributors, clients and consumers. Training of suppliers can be very varied, as it may cover quality standards, health and safety regulations, use of computer systems and software, and factory or operational centre visits to meet opposite numbers.

3.13 CONCLUSION

Organizing for quality is very much within the remit of leaders at every level. It is their role to identify what form of organization works best for them in serving the customer and the management implications of adopting one form rather than another. They have to be alert to how these structures may need to evolve and grow according to how quality is progressing in the organization itself and the feedback it is receiving from its customers. What is of interest is that structures and systems are of key importance in supporting the people at the interface who deliver quality. How well these are resourced and deployed depends on leadership at every level of the organization. How effective they are depends on how they are helped by the culture.

ACTION QUESTIONS

- How effective is your current organization structure in helping to deliver quality?
- How often do you review it and its supporting systems?
- How comprehensive is the feedback on customer care within your organization? Does it reach the people who are committed to taking action?

REFERENCES

1 Clark, F.A. (1992): *Total Career Management*, McGraw-Hill, Maidenhead, UK.
2 Carlzon, J. (1987): *Moments of Truth*, Ballinger Publishing Company, Wisconsin, USA.
3 Krackhardt, D. and Hanson, J.R. (1993): 'Informal Networks: the Company Behind the Chart', *Harvard Business Review*, July–August, pp. 104–19.
4 Senge, P.M. (1990): *The Fifth Discipline*, Doubleday, New York, USA.
5 Garvin, D.A. (1993): 'Building a Learning Organization', *Harvard Business Review*, July–August, pp. 78–91.
6 Maryland Centre for Quality and Productivity (1986): *Organizational Quality and Productivity Self Audit*, University of Maryland, College of Business and Management, College Park, MD, USA.
7 Sheffield, D.T., Godkin, L. and Drapeau, R. (1993): 'An Industry Specific Study of Factors Contributing to the Maintenance and Longevity of

Quality Circles', *British Journal of Management*, **4**(1), pp. 47–55.

8 Zeithaml, V.A., Berry, L.L. and Parasuraman, A. (1993): 'The Nature and Determinants of Customer Expectations of Service', *Journal of the Academy of Marketing Science*, **21**(1), pp. 1–12.

9 Stalk, G, and Webber, A.M. (1993): 'Japan's Dark Side of Time', *Harvard Business Review*, July–August, pp. 93–102.

10 Evans, D. (1993): 'Hewlett Packard Users Slam Quality of Support', *Computer Weekly*, 4 November, p. 5.

11 Reicheld, F.F. and Sasser, W.E. (1990): 'Zero Defections: Quality Comes to Services, *Harvard Business Review*, September/October 1990, pp. 105–11.

12 Reicheld, F.F. and Sasser, W.E. (1990), op. cit.

13 Sherden, W.A. (1988): 'Gaining the Service Quality Advantage', *Journal of Business Strategy*, March/April, pp. 45–8.

A culture receptive to quality

4.1 INTRODUCTION

As we have seen in the preceding chapters, the decision to adopt quality as a way of life within the organization implies a certain approach to the way it conducts its business. The CEO will have a key influence on the supporting values, attitudes, norms and sanctions which all combine to give an organization its distinctive culture. A model for diagnosing culture has been developed by the author as shown in Fig. 4.1.

An explanation of the terms is important here, since managers often talk about culture as being 'informal', 'soft', 'invisible', and the 'glue which holds the organization together'. The aspects of my model may seem like this, but they, too, can be measured and monitored.

The five building blocks of culture are shown to the left of the diagram. First, any organization has to identify its *symbols*. These are objects, acts, relationships which represent a variety of meanings, evoke emotions and drive people to action. Corporate logos and national flags are some familiar examples. These symbols are emotionally charged and are the means by which a group or organization represents its situation to itself and to the outside world. In the UK, Big Ben symbolizes parliament which, in turn, stands for democratic government. The Disney Corporation has 'the Mouse' which represents childhood fantasy, leisure and enjoyment, the reason for the corporation's existence. Some NHS trusts have badges to show that they have BS5750.

Language helps to stabilize and communicate our experiences to give them personal and social meaning. It provides an organization's or nation's historical and cultural heritage and may also impel people to action, since it

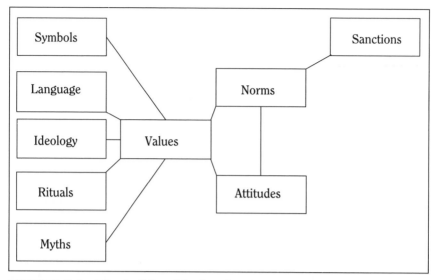

FIGURE 4.1 **The building blocks of corporate and national culture**

contains social exhortation and evaluations. Therefore the analysis of vocabularies is an important source of information about organizations, as it provides details about the expressed meaning of organizational life. In Disneyland, there is an extended metaphor of the theatre which conveys the ideas and values embodied in entertaining customers. People are 'cast' for a role in the show; employees are 'performers' on a 'stage' (the theme park). They are 'hosts' to the 'guests' (not customers) and 'costumes' (not uniforms) are issued to 'cast members' (not staff) who 'take a break backstage' when they are off duty. In some organizations, slogans declaim: Quality matters and quality is everybody's business.

An *ideology* is a set of beliefs about the social world and how it operates. It contains statements about the 'rightness' of certain social arrangements and what actions should be taken in the light of those views. The ideology (or philosophy) has a part to play in the formation of organizational processes because it has the potential to link attitude and action. Ideologies link social obligations with general ethical principles. Statements such as 'The customer is always right' produce certain behaviours. The statements of values which many organizations have mutually reinforce each other to provide a coherent ideology. In Disneyland, the philosophy towards the customer is to 'entertain them and give them a good time'. In other sectors, for example, the commercial decision to withdraw all products when a few have been shown to be potentially dangerous or unsatisfactory is linked back to the ideology of the organization. At 3M, corporate risk and innovation are encouraged, as is the fact that 15 per cent of time and resources go into bootlegging for new technology. Corporate lawlessness (up to a point) is thus tolerated to keep one step ahead.

Ritual is often thought of in a derogatory way, being seen as a series of repetitive actions without any meaning. However, it is important in social situations because it conveys a message and gives people a rationale for behaving in the way they do. It may also convey exclusivity, as those that know the ritual are the 'insiders'. Rituals are seen on a national level as special holidays, or at an organizational level, for example, as celebrations of quality (see Chapter 5). There is also an acknowledged ritual in 3M, the makers of the 'Post-it' note and the compact disc. There, product innovation follows an accepted pattern. The product champion has to make a presentation to a group of senior managers and directors (who have themselves successfully been through this process). The test is a form of 'rites of passage', and if successful in gaining agreement to a new product, the event marks for the manager a transition into the 'heroes' club' at 3M. Rituals draw attention to the importance of quality in organizational life. British Gas has its 'Gold Flame' award and Royal Mail has its Team event (see Chapter 5).

Myths are also suspect in lay terms as unbelievable stories, held without any substantial evidence. In organizational life they serve to highlight 'heroic' deeds, with people doing the impossible. Product champions become part of the mythology at 3M because they have done something outstanding. The ordinary members of an organization who receive quality awards for, perhaps, an unusual dedication and persistence in satisfying a customer, become part of the organizational folklore.

All these five elements give clues about what is important to an organization, or indeed, nation; that is to say, its values. They reinforce each other or direct attention to its purpose. Supposing all these five elements point to customer service or quality as an important value. The norms, sanctions and attitudes should then be related to them in some way that is consistent. The norm (which represents the standards of behaviour expected) might be that 'The customer is always right' or that 'We are never offhand with customers' and certainly never show anger. There will also be sanctions in the organization to enforce these norms and values. The positive one will be that people are rewarded for good attitudes and behaviour towards the customer and the negative one will be perhaps a low performance rating at appraisal time and possibly no salary increase if they are discourteous. Attitudes may exist towards the values themselves, and may be positive (I like our approach to putting the customer first) or negative (I think the customer care programme is a waste of time). They may also exist towards the object of those values (this place would run smoothly if it weren't for those customers making unreasonable demands). They may also be directed towards the norms (I don't think we should be expected to have to keep our tempers with rude customers). Altering any of the values, norms, sanctions or attitudes will impact on the culture. That is where the CEO has the power to help change the culture.

4.2 THE CEO AS LEADER

The culture is articulated at all levels in the organization, but very powerfully and visibly by its CEO and sometimes its chairman. Companies where the CEOs are very visible and supportive champions are Corning, Ford and Xerox. The importance of a clear resolve to make things work[1] is given by James Houghton, chairman and CEO of Corning Glass:

> When you dive into quality, a lot of people are standing on the beach, waiting to see if the water is too cold. Waiting to see if you turn blue and climb right back out again. If you do, they will not even dip their toes in the water.

He continues by saying that this visibility takes 'real work'. Each year he visits some 50 Corning facilities around the world, a major theme being quality.

Bill Coburn of the Post Office, who masterminded the revolution in quality at Royal Mail, is another high-profile CEO. As he has said throughout the changes: 'Success is cheaper than failure'.

He communicates his message using all the media at his command. In the major times of change, company-wide videos link the person with the message, so that there is no doubt as to who is the face behind the words.

Jack Welch of General Electric has set a role model for quality[2] so that people will ask their bosses:

Why do you require me to do these wasteful things? Why don't you let me do the things you shouldn't be doing so you can move on and create? That's the job of a leader – to create, not control. Trust me to do my job and don't make me waste all my time trying to deal with you on the control issue.

This has been the inspiration for 'Workout', where the practical aim has been to eliminate bad work habits which have become custom and practice. The intellectual part is to expose business leaders about 8–10 times a year to their people: 'to the vibrations of their business – opinions, feelings, emotions, resentments, not abstract theories of organizations and management'.

Leadership for quality is about listening and learning.

In a survey of CEOs[3], it was found that less than one quarter saw themselves as 'standard bearers for quality'. This could have been achieved by adopting a high-profile role in raising quality awareness, helping to develop a quality culture, acting as quality improvement leader or by chairing appropriate committees. Just over 30 per cent said that they were totally involved in quality management on a day-to-day basis, acting as a focal point for quality by creating and maintaining a quality culture within their organization. It was also reported that as the prime internal change agent (see Chapter 8) the CEO had two main roles: shaping the values of the organization; and creating a managerial infrastructure to bring about that change. The real task of the CEO is to generate fundamental commitment to change. Alterations in methods or procedures may be generated by compliance, but commitment is needed if transformational changes to the core mission, values and strategy of an organization are to take place. Some examples are offered in the next section.

4.3 ORGANIZATIONAL MISSION

It is now part of conventional organizational thinking that it is fundamental to have a mission statement to highlight the nature and purpose of the organization. Basically, it is answering the question 'What are we here for?' Simplistic statements such as 'to make a profit' are no longer adequate, since an organization has many different stakeholders and its mission is linked to a set of values implicitly or explicitly (see below). Organizations such as BP, Cyanamid, Johnson and Johnson, Royal Mail and Rank Xerox all have them. Their clarity, utility and comprehensiveness may vary, and

To provide world-class telecommunications and information products
and services and to develop and exploit our networks at home and
overseas.

(British Telecom)

To meet customer needs faster, better, more distinctively.

(Courtaulds)

An impeccable and positive image with the consumer, a unique franchise
system second to none, and the intimate knowledge of and contacts with
local business conditions around the world.

(Coca Cola)

To invest in good quality basic businesses providing essential goods
and services for the consumer and industry.

(Hanson)

FIGURE 4.2   Mission statements

the cynics might say that they are bland statements of the obvious, but a
number of mission statements are given in Fig. 4.2 as illustrations.
However, the need for mission statements is strongly supported by
management gurus[4]:

> That business purpose and business mission are so rarely given adequate
> thought is perhaps the most important cause of business frustration and failure.

From this perspective, a mission statement is a crucial base for any business
strategy since it asks the fundamental questions: 'What business are we in?'
and 'What business should we be in?' While some may criticize mission
statements as being too general, they do focus the intellectual, physical and
emotional energy of organizations. Their generality is their strength, as it
allows individuals at different levels and functions within the organization
to identify their jobs within it. At the Rover site in Cowley, Oxford, different
departments have adapted the overall mission and values statements to
reflect more closely their local operation. These statements are proudly
displayed at entrances and exits to departments and within work areas. The
visitor cannot avoid seeing them and recognizing the subtle shifts from one
area to another.

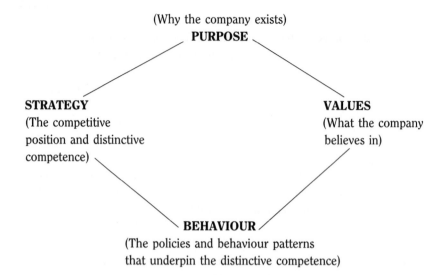

(Why the company exists)
PURPOSE

STRATEGY
(The competitive
position and distinctive
competence)

VALUES
(What the company
believes in)

BEHAVIOUR
(The policies and behaviour patterns
that underpin the distinctive competence)

FIGURE 4.3   A model for a mission

Source: A. Campbell and S. Yeung. Reproduced with permission from the
Journal of Long Range Planning, Vol. 24, No. 4, 1991

One useful framework for writing mission statements[5] is given in Fig.
4.3. First, it identifies three categories of organizations according to
purpose:

- those satisfying their shareholders (for example, Hanson)
- those satisfying their stakeholders (for example, Monsanto)
- those for both and some higher ideal (for example, Marks and Spencer).

The authors suggest that purposes which focus on the first two tend to
elicit self-centred interests, whereas the third type is more likely to bind the
organization together.

The second element is the strategy. If, for example, the intention is to
be the leader in the field, there needs to be an indication of the way in
which it can be done. One of Grand Metropolitan's annual reports says that
'its style is about winning – never satisfied and always innovative'.

Thirdly, there are behaviour standards. These are vital if the aims are
to be embodied in the operation of the organization.

Fourthly, what holds all this together is a set of values, which will be
dealt with in the next section. The authors maintain that when all four parts
of the mission are in harmony, the company will have a strong sense of
mission. However, even when there is a strong mission there will always be

individuals who do not commit themselves. That is why it is important to conduct regular attitude surveys to sense the atmosphere and see where potential causes of discontent may lie.

4.4 CREATING THE VALUES

The mission of an organization will influence its values. Companies often have slogans which encapsulate their purpose and draw attention to the underlying values ('IBM means service' or Chubb Insurance's 'Underwriting excellence'). In both these examples the issue is service quality. With General Electric ('Progress is our most important product'), the focus is on the value of creativity and innovation. The mission of an organization cannot be delivered unless people share certain values about why and how it is to be done. That is why these often go hand in hand. Royal Mail (Fig. 4.4) displays its business values prominently around the organization for employees and visitors alike.

We each care about:

- Our customers and their requirements for:
  Reliability
  Value for money
  Accessibility
  Courtesy
  Integrity
  Security
  Prompt and timely response
- All our fellow employees and their needs for:
  Respect
  Training and development
  Involvement
  Recognition and rewards
- The way we do our job and the way it affects our customers both inside and outside the business
- Our role in the life of the community

We are proud to be part of Royal Mail

FIGURE 4.4 Royal Mail business values

The business	
Lean	critical to develop world cost leadership
Agile	to create fast decision making
Creative	to create customer satisfaction and operating margins
Ownership	supports concept of individual responsibility
Reward	recognition and compensation to attract and motivate people who will achieve the objectives. A first-class business should provide first-class people with first-class opportunities
Individual	
Reality	describe the environment as it is, not as we hope it to be; a critical factor in developing a vision
Leadership	to rally teams towards a common objective
Candour/openness	frequent information sharing so employees know where they stand
Simplicity	less complexity improves everything
Integrity	live within both the spirit and the letter of the laws of every global business area
Individual dignity	respect for the talent and contribution of individuals since teamwork depends on trust, understanding and belief that the individual will be treated fairly in any environment

FIGURE 4.5   General Electric's business values

These mission and value statements are usually offered in the form of a printed, credit-card-sized, laminated card available for reference and to guide daily behaviour.

Another set of values are those of General Electric (GE) (given in Fig. 4.5 with a shortened form of explanation) which relate to the business. For each one there is a 'what' and 'why' explanation which are not shown here.

In developing this statement of corporate values, GE took three years and some 5000 people were consulted in the process. Not a task for the uncommitted!

At Levi Strauss, the clothing manufacturer, its chairman and CEO Robert Haas believes that a company's values are crucial to achieving competitive success[6] and shows how they are linked to leadership:

> In a more volatile and dynamic business environment the controls have to be conceptual. They can't be human any more ... It's the ideas of a business that

are controlling, not some manager with authority. Values provide a common language for aligning a company's leadership and its people.

While it used to be thought that strategy created that alignment, a strategy will not work if people do not believe in it, as Levi Strauss found to its cost in the 1980s when it followed a principle of diversification and acquisition. It then reverted to its core business and reshaped it according to the strategy and values. Levi Strauss has produced a statement of aspirations (values) which is reproduced in a shortened form in Fig. 4.6.

'We all want a company that our people are proud of and committed to, where the employees have an opportunity to contribute, learn and grow and advance based on merit not on politics or background. We want our people to feel respected, treated fairly, listened to and involved. Above all we want satisfaction from accomplishments and friendships, balanced personal and professional lives and to have fun in our endeavours.'

FIGURE 4.6   Aspirations statement (Levi Strauss)

The aspirations statement also contains guidelines about what kind of leadership is necessary to make them a reality (not given here). The value of these aspirations has been in decision making, challenging plant closures, for example, and the effects on individuals and the community. It also forces people to slow down, reflect and weigh up all the factors before rushing in. The aspirations drive the business, not the other way round. To be most effective, these need to be supported by quality policies.

4.5 QUALITY POLICIES

The strategic reasons for taking the quality route need to be consistent with the overall mission statement and values of the organization. These may need alteration to avoid inconsistency or to add emphasis. Quality policies should then follow from the mission and be grounded in the cultural values of the organization. Quality policies are vital for organizations to develop a sustainable quality culture. They are the way in which mission and values are translated into actions, and guide and help to order and prioritize the many improvement programmes which may be suggested. A recent survey[7] of CEOs showed that only 41 per cent had a published quality policy and approximately 25 per cent had a recognized quality system. However, having a clearly defined and articulated policy was also a characteristic of companies which had been successful in introducing TQM. NatWest's quality policy comprises four main headings, and the value statements are shown in Fig. 4.7.

The NatWest way is to bring:
Quality to our customers. We value our customers as the foundation of our business.
Quality to our investors. We have a long-term responsibility to everybody who has a stake in the group to operate with care, efficiency and at a profit.
Quality to our people. We respect each other's experience and skills and value the contribution each of us makes to the NatWest team.
Quality to the community. We recognize that our actions must acknowledge our responsibilities for the wellbeing and stability of the community. We aim to support the community through the involvement of our people and the contribution of 1 per cent of our Group profits.

FIGURE 4.7 NatWest's quality value statements

Leadership Through Quality, Rank Xerox's programme, is based on the following statement, which in 1983 formed the basis of a complete cultural change[8] (Fig. 4.8).

Xerox is a quality company. Quality is the basic business principle for Xerox. Quality means providing our internal and external customers with innovative products and services that fully satisfy their requirements. Quality improvement is the job of every Xerox employee.

FIGURE 4.8 Rank Xerox's statement of quality

The quality statements are not over-elaborate. The important thing is that they convey simply and clearly what quality means for the organization, so that actions can be taken and understood in a context which is relevant to the customer and internal staff.

4.6 AVOIDING THE FAILURE TRAP

In Chapter 2 mention was made of the cynicism that may develop when quality programmes fail to deliver the promised and hoped for results (Chapter 1, 1.10). The process has been likened to a 'rain dance'[9] where: 'managers continue to dance round and round the camp fire, exuding faith and dissipating energy' in the hope that some good will come of it in the end.

Programmes typically include a new management style, empowerment, benchmarking and customer satisfaction. The assumption is that if all these activities are undertaken all will be well. Expectations are set high, quality will deliver. The danger is that these initiatives start by focusing on processes and not on the results they are designed to achieve and then determining whether quality, or another driver, is the way forward. The activity-centred programmes are, according to this analysis, likely to fail for the following reasons:

- *not keyed to specific results* (managers do not specify which performance indicators they wish to improve and rarely make explicit how the activity will lead to the result);
- *too large-scale and diffuse* (they launch a wide range of activities together with so many programmes that they cannot tell which are working);
- *results are taboo* (managers do not like to say that they cannot see results in case they are accused of short-termism; the expectation is that things are always long-term, painful and that culture change takes time);
- *delusional measurement* (false equation of measures of activity with measurement of results. The Baldridge Award gives only 180 points to this);
- *staff- and consultant-driven* (managers have exhausted their own ideas for improvement);
- *bias towards orthodoxy, not empiricism* (approach based on faith rather than learning from experience. Too many improvement teams can have counter-productive results, taking people away from core businesses).

By contrast, the key benefits of results-driven programmes are said to be:

- companies use management process innovations only as required (forcing careful prioritization of goals on a 'just in time' basis);
- empirical testing reveals what works (rather than blind acceptance);

- frequent reinforcement energizes the improvement process (short-term incremental projects give feedback);
- continuous learning process (built into lessons of previous stages; each project is a testing ground).

The approach is, if you can't measure it you can't manage it.

Perhaps this approach is best exemplified by GE's 'Workout' process across the organization, which is dealt with in the next chapter. In terms of avoiding the pitfalls, and reflecting on his experiences, the managing director of Leyland Daf is reported to have said[10]:

> Quality improvement is not easy – if it were we could have implemented it a long while ago .... It is quicker to do it correctly than to do it twice.

The last word on the causes of failure is with Cyanamid's booklet for its staff. The five reasons why things are said to go wrong in business are: the requirements are not clear; they are not taken seriously by management; they are not communicated; the work process is not capable of delivering the required result; and the people are not trained. The message is that if staff have a quality problem, it will be one or more of these and, most frequently, the first one. This begins to focus their minds on looking at the system rather than seeking causes in clashes of personality.

4.7 THE QUALITY SCHOOL

Once the organization's senior managers have examined their mission, values and policies and have thought about avoiding the quality trap, a useful action is to develop their own quality school so that they are continuously updating themselves and their thinking on quality to see whether their approaches need alteration.

Shell is a good exponent of this type of thinking. In 1987 the company formed its school for the top management cadre. It set about bringing new ideas into the company in a systematic way and invited gurus and managers from other organizations to give their views and experience. The company was then in a better position to pick and choose those aspects of quality programmes which might be of greater significance to its own culture. Royal Mail has an informal network of people who arrange lunchtime seminars about topics of interest or approaches which have been tried out internally. It also invites outside speakers to seminars on a more infrequent basis.

4.8 QUALITY DEVELOPMENT AUDIT

A culture receptive to quality has to conduct an audit to find out first in general terms how an organization sees its own performance in relation to quality. The various quality awards described in Chapters 6 and 9 have specific criteria which, in several cases, can be used as a self-assessment audit. They will therefore not be discussed here. One method of doing an audit[11] is to see in which quality 'era' the organization is operating. According to that perspective, there are four such eras depending on the general approach to how quality is introduced and maintained in the organization:

I   *Inspection* (quality is inspected in)

II   *Quality control* (quality is controlled in)

III   *Quality assurance* (quality is built in)

IV   *Strategic quality management* (quality is managed in).

Each era can be assessed against the seven criteria on a continuum whose ranges are given below:

1 *Primary concern* (detection of quality rather than concern for its strategic impact).

2 *View of quality* (problem to be solved instead of a competitive opportunity).

3 *Emphasis* (uniformity of products or services rather than meeting diverse customer needs).

4 *Methods* (gauging existing situation instead of planning and mobilization).

5 *Role of quality professionals* (inspection and sorting rather than education, consulting and programme design).

6 *Responsibility for quality* (inspection department rather than the concern of all the staff).

7 *Approach* (quality is inspected in rather than managed in).

It is this last criterion which is the fundamental differentiator. When groups of managers are asked to assess in which era they think their organization is operating, they may be surprised to find that there is not as much consistency as might have been expected. For example, at a general level few believe they are truly in a strategic era. A further complication is that they feel their organizations might be at different points along the continuum of the seven criteria. An example of these dilemmas is that the current organizational view of quality may be that it is a competitive opportunity (strategic era IV), but the responsibility for quality rests within a specific department (quality control era I) and the role of quality professionals is restricted to measurement, planning and programme design (quality assurance era III). Nevertheless, the exercise is seen as very thought-provoking and perhaps useful in explaining why quality programmes are not having the desired impact. As such, it can offer a way forward for the organization.

Another approach[12] is to examine closely the organization's

- customers
- people
- management
- business processes.

Customer surveys (see Chapter 3) will provide excellent feedback. The real issue is how willing the organization is to listen (even if the criticism seems unfounded) and to decide how to deal with it. It may be the case that administrative convenience has overtaken the needs of the customer.

Employee attitude surveys (see Chapter 5) are now becoming a regular part of organizational life. These are important in order to see what satisfaction and commitment exist regarding the organization and its customers and to identify where special efforts need to be made. Satisfaction alone does not necessarily imply commitment. The surveys are also crucial in determining what kind of culture is actually in operation (for example, the use of particular management styles, the adoption of organization-wide standards, attitudes to problem solving and innovation). The reader will see that all these topics are covered in subsequent sections. These survey findings will suggest gaps between the existing situation and the desired one. This provides an agenda for improvement in terms of how educated, motivated and involved people are in working for quality.

On the management front, it is important to identify how able they are to set objectives and manage performance related to quality, otherwise any initiatives will not succeed. How capable are they of adopting new ideas? How well do they coordinate resources and facilitate their team's effort? What communication processes do they use and how effective are they?

Leadership by example is also important, and the leadership charter of Royal Mail has already been mentioned in Chapter 1 as an indication of how crucial this is to the support of a quality strategy.

With regard to business processes, it is important to know whether they are mapped, understood by those who use them and effectively monitored and subject to continuous review to see if they are working effectively. The key here is to select the ones which are crucial to the business and at a suitable level of detail to identify the main decision points. The subject of business process re-engineering will be covered in Chapter 9.

A third approach is to conduct a problems audit. This may include complaints, product recalls, warranty or amount of scrap produced to identify where the organization needs to focus its efforts by ranking them against corporate objectives (e.g. market share or profitability). There are also a number of criteria[13] which help to assess whether an organization is ready for quality:

- management understanding or attitude
- quality organization and status
- problem identification and prevention
- control of costs of quality
- quality improvement actions.

Whichever framework is chosen, the benefits of a quality audit are that the different components can be linked together to form a basis to evaluate quality initiatives, identify weaknesses and assess the actions to be taken to improve a product or service.

Another analysis[14] shows what the pressures are for quality and its audit. These revolve around the replacement of:

- real time controls with ex-post audits
- professional discretion with precisely defined contract
- judgement by numbers
- shift of power to the users.

These thoughts are summed up in the following quote from the same source:

> Distrust (between individuals and institutions) undermines the old assumptions of professional autonomy and fuels the spread of audits, performance measurements and other means of external control.

These imperatives, coupled with spending constraints and the public hunger for information and league tables, all drive organizations to attempt to measure their quality, if only because those making comparisons will want to know why the figures cannot be produced.

Institutions themselves also provide an anchoring point for audit. For example, there are many self-regulatory bodies such as the Securities Investment Board, the Advertising Standards Authority, the Press Complaints Commission, which are self-funding, thereby ensuring independence from direct government intervention.

The success of any audit depends on the clarity of purpose of the organization's existence in the first place. The current confusion and heated debates in the higher education system in the UK exemplifies this problem. One viewpoint suggests that its purpose is to produce employable graduates; a second, that it is there to produce student satisfaction; and a third, that the main purpose is the dissemination of knowledge. This is why there is much complaint about the duplication of effort in meeting the demands of the Higher Education Funding Council (government-owned) and the Higher Education Quality Council (university-owned).

4.9 LEADERSHIP STYLE

The willingness to acknowledge problems arising out of audits depends on a suitable leadership style, as was emphasized in the turnaround of Scandinavian Airline System (SAS). If there is a need for continuous improvement and constant striving there must be a willingness to embrace certain behaviours. As the CEO said[15]:

> A leader, then, is a person who is oriented towards results more than power or social relations. Someone seeking power for its own sake may well sacrifice both the personal relationship and results to obtain it.

Of course, those who are too socially oriented may feel that they have to avoid conflict and compromise at every turn, which can also harm results. The other part of this behaviour means that the leader will not attempt to dictate methods for achieving these results.

Secondly, the leader does not need to take credit for all the successes. Nothing is more demoralizing for staff than not to receive credit for ideas, having been called upon to share them in the first place. This kind of behaviour shows that the leaders are insecure in the value of their own contributions and not concerned to develop their staff. As the CEO said: 'Good ideas flow freely from every division of the company and are all channelled towards the same company-wide vision.'

Thirdly, the role is to serve, not instruct. This is done when managers understand their department's objectives and have the information and resources to meet them. This change has to be handled sensitively. At SAS it was said that the middle managers had not been given an alternative to their previous role as rule interpreters and did not know what their new behaviour should be. Managers in a TQM environment need a coaching and facilitating style to bring out people's full potential. The difficulty is that many of the senior managers in organizations have reached their position through using a traditional style and may find it hard to change to the new way of doing things.

The last word on this matter should come from Rank Xerox's 'Leadership through Quality', which also summarizes this section:

> ... it does not matter how cleverly crafted the words are if they are at odds with the way managers behave ... the most effective means of communication is management behaviour.

People model themselves on behaviour seen to be rewarded, and that shapes the culture.

4.10 CREATING ORGANIZATIONAL STANDARDS

Creating organizational standards is itself a key lever in producing a culture geared to delivering quality. Equally, a culture which is receptive to improving quality is more readily able to identify standards and evolve and accept them for themselves rather than feeling that they have been imposed from the top.

At SAS, standards were traditionally given by top management and underwent various forms of transformation via middle managers. Ambiguity was welcomed, as it allowed leeway in the trade-off between quality and costs. Within the flatter, more decentralized organization, employees at all levels need to know exactly what the organization requires and how decisions are affecting what is achieved.

In a service-oriented organization, the ability to set relevant, quantitative goals is crucial. If they are subject to so many external factors that they demoralize those who pursue them. For example, those involved in the policy formulation of road safety would find difficulty in relating their performance to the reduction of accidents and in assessing the quality of their output.

However, an attempt has to be made to define organizational goals and a standard acceptable to clients and customers. For example, if, in various parts of the public sector services, there were ten rail crashes, ten babies dropped in maternity units or ten gas explosions, this would be a cause for public alarm. If the following year's plan was to reduce this by 50 per cent, this would still be seen as unsatisfactory. Why? Because in this sector the public has come to expect a standard of performance which is 'zero defects', even though a 50 per cent improvement in performance from one year to another would be seen as a magnificent effort in other organizations.

The cultural message which derives from this is that goals must shift towards the 'zero defects' standard. While some might think that this is an impossible task, the counter-argument is that if this does not happen, nothing will be achieved. The organizational compromise is to try to raise standards in manageable stages to avoid demoralization in trying to bridge a seemingly enormous gap. Royal Mail has done this and continues to strive for improvement in the delivery of its first class mail. When its quality programmes began in 1988, the 'next day delivery' performance was 74.5 per cent; two years later it was 85.5 per cent; and is currently running at 93 per cent.

If standards are to spread throughout the organization, a useful lever is to know where they come from. As well as the environmental pressures previously mentioned, there are the customers, the competition, regulatory bodies, managers and their staff. The information is there if everybody listens. Customers can influence the standards directly through increasingly demanding specifications and by voicing complaints or suggestions made directly to the organization. They can also influence them indirectly by withdrawing their custom, and telling the competition and the regulatory bodies. This latter group can affect standards through their usual controls, direct or indirect accreditation, funding or legislation.

Organization-wide standards are difficult to achieve. First, in order to create and sustain them, there needs to be agreement as to what they are through a process of shared understanding before suitable measures can be derived. Employees will need to consider the meaning of this for the organization and assess the impact on their jobs. The process can cause anxiety, since it will not be possible to know in advance what the effects are, and those which are known may not be palatable. Secondly, acceptance of some standards, such as 'zero defects' or 'right first time', may seem impossible to achieve, and if this is suggested straightaway it will only cause people to become demoralized. Thirdly, if suitable measures of performance and quality are to be found, Deming's tenet 'drive out fear' has to apply, as only then will staff be amenable to identifying suitable measures and the circumstances that can affect these being achieved.

There are other ways in which organizational standards can be created. Benchmarking against external sources is one method. However, this is a separate topic on its own and is covered in Chapter 6. Independent accreditation and awards such as the ISO 9000 standard and the European Foundation for Quality Management (EFQM) is another. Finally, training is a way of ensuring that the standards are communicated (see next chapter).

4.11 PROBLEM SOLVING FOR QUALITY

A fundamental part of a culture which is receptive to quality is its willingness and ability to actively seek out problems (a fuller discussion of problem solving and innovation is given in Chapters 7 and 9). This usually involves a major shift from traditional views that problems are what bosses do not want to hear about. This can be particularly difficult when individuals need to be presenting a successful face to their peers and to other parts of the organization.

Companies which are deemed successful at delivering quality (Sir John Harvey Jones has gone on record as pointing to British Airways, Rover and ICL) recognize that in the search for continuous improvement, there will certainly be problems. Companies such as these provide their staff with as many tools as possible to help achieve this end.

British Airways issues a pocket booklet as a guide for continuous improvement groups based on the 'FADE' technique (focus, analyse, develop, execute) which represents the four stages. Each phase has a stated output, the necessary steps and a selection of tools to help in the process:

- *Focus* (choose a problem and describe it).
- *Analyse* (learn about the problem from data).
- *Develop* (develop a solution and plan).
- *Execute* (implement plan, monitor results and adjust as necessary).

All these stages are then further elaborated. For example, in verifying the definition of the problem, other questions arise: Is it important enough to be worth the effort? How widespread is it? How does it affect people?

British Telecom has an approach to focusing its problem solving for quality called 'tackling the tails'. The rationale is that efforts are concentrated on those areas which are performing the worst (the tails) rather than looking at the averages. This has the effect of raising the overall quality of service by cancelling out the effect of the worst performance.

4.12 INNOVATION AND QUALITY

Once the culture has accepted the problem-solving mode as a way forward for continuous improvement, the questions shift from being totally reactive to being proactive. This involves a self-critical approach to the existing organization as well as a sensitivity to what consumers will be asking for next and an eye for changes in technology or delivery mechanisms which will extend everyone's horizons. In fact, major innovation requires a paradigm shift. Since strategic management is concerned with following an accepted paradigm, any new ideas will fail unless they can be reinterpreted and reconstructed in terms of another newly accepted paradigm. If not, these novel ideas are seen as threatening the very existence of political élites who have formed the current culture (see Chapter 8 on working within the power structure).

The spur to this is often customer-driven (see Chapter 9 for a discussion of this approach). Many organizations make a point of keeping very close to the customer as well as immediately tracking any kind of dissatisfaction in order to pick up ideas which can be turned to their advantage in differentiating their product or service. To this end, BA has a departmental league table for brainstorming ideas. To avoid duplication, directors are creating a company-wide collation of ideas so that recurring themes can be identified.

4.13 CONCLUSION

The culture which is receptive to quality has an atmosphere or feel about it. People want to meet your request; if there is an error or late appointment it embarrasses the staff, they are anxious to make good and stress that the mistake is at odds with their values. The aim of any cultural programme will be to embed quality in all activities to the point where it is not a separate aspect of performance – it is the performance itself. As Levi Strauss, the anthropologist, said: 'The most important thing to know about a culture is what it takes for granted.'

ACTION QUESTIONS

- Have you the means to diagnose what kind of culture exists in your organization?
- Are your values visible? Do you check that they are guiding behaviour?
- Is there a recognizable managerial style and does it support quality?

REFERENCES

1 Houghton, J.R. (1991): 'World Class Quality', *Total Quality Management*, February, pp. 27–31.

2 Ticky, N. and Charan, R. (1989): 'Speed, Simplicity, and Self-confidence: An interview with Jack Welsh', *Harvard Business Review*, September/October, pp. 112–20.

3 Lascelles, D. and Dale, B. (1990): 'Quality Management: The Chief Executive's Perception and the Role', *European Management Journal*, **8**(1), March, pp. 67–75.

4 Drucker, P.F. (1973): *Management: Tasks, Responsibilities, and Practices*, Harper and Row, New York, USA.

5 Campbell, A. and Yeung, S. (1991): 'Creating a Sense of Mission', *Long Range Planning*, **24**(4), pp. 10–20.

6 Howard, R. (1990): 'Values Make The Company. An interview with Robert Haas', *Harvard Business Review*, September/October, pp. 133–44.

7 Lascelles, D. and Dale, B. (1990), op. cit.

8 Walker, R. (1992): 'Rank Xerox–Management Revolution.' *Long Range Planning*, **25**(1), pp. 9–21.

9 Schaffer, R.H. and Thompson, H.A. (1992): 'Successful Change Programmes Begin with Results', *Harvard Business Review*, January/February, pp. 80–9.

10 Chase, R. (1990): 'Working Together', *Total Quality Management Magazine*, **2**(4), August, pp. 221–4.

11 Garvin, D.A. (1990): 'Competing Through Quality', *Harvard Business School Video Series*, Harvard Business School, Boston, USA.

12 Wythe, R. (1990): 'Agenda for Change', *Total Quality Management Magazine*, **2**(4), August, pp. 209–16.

13 Crosby, P.B. (1979): *Quality is Free*, McGraw-Hill, New York, USA.

14 Mulgan, G. (1993): 'Judging by Numbers', *Times Higher Educational Supplement*, p. 21.

15 Carlzon, J. (1987): *Moments of Truth*, Ballinger Publishing Company, USA.

CHAPTER 5

Organizational policies and processes for quality

5.1 INTRODUCTION

While consistency of strategy, structure and culture are fundamental to support organizations along the road to quality, they need to be formally underpinned by sound policies and processes if quality is to become a way of life. Enthusiasm and commitment will soon disappear if processes are not in place to influence and reinforce the culture. It will be noted that the policies and processes covered in this chapter are oriented towards people. In ICL's recent turnaround, the capability of its people was deemed to be the critical differentiator and it has recently won the European Foundation for Quality Management Award.

Choosing the title for this chapter posed some questions. At first, it read 'Human resources policies and processes', since many of these areas within organizations are driven by that function. However, several of them, even if directly coordinated by the human resources (HR) function, rely on line management for their effectiveness. On the other hand, quality and customer care programmes, which may be championed by the quality director, steering committees, and line management, depend on strong inputs from the HR function. Within ICL, the HR function played a strategic role in the company's cultural revolution by ensuring that its core values and quality awareness were spread throughout all its training programmes.

Nevertheless, HR does have an important role to play in this area. A recent survey[1] conducted for the then Institute of Personnel Management (now the Institute of Personnel and Development) showed that 76 per cent of the responding organizations who had experience of quality management reported that the HR function played a role in the implementation of quality. Of the many roles highlighted, important ones were facilitation, cultural change and training. The report stated that:

> quality management can be instrumental in promoting a consultancy role for HR practitioners, in which they advise and guide general management and supervisors who are increasingly having to apply HR skills to their everyday activities.

It was also found that, where HR specialists were involved in quality management at a strategic level, organizations were more likely to view quality as a process of continuous improvement. Leaders at every level therefore have the ability to influence these policies through their actual or desired effects on their day-to-day activity. Human Resources in turn are keen to develop their role and be seen as adding value to the business.

5.2 RECOGNITION

Any quality improvement programme has to begin with whatever resources are available, and that is why this chapter does not begin with recruitment, but with individuals being motivated to work for continuous improvement. Recognition, as covered here, is non-monetary and does not mean benefits in kind. For example, every manager and every colleague has the capability to give recognition where it is due and to say 'thank you' – a behaviour of which Cyanamid, the pharmaceutical company, continually reminds its people.

Air Products, the international supplier of industrial gases, chemicals and process equipment, has been involved in total quality since 1985. Every attendee on its quality awareness workshops receives a certificate and badge as a sign of his or her knowledge of, and belief in, quality. It has instigated its own European Quality Improvement Award, which gives formal recognition of up to five awards of exceptional instances of quality improvement, either on an individual or team basis for outstanding projects. The winners are chosen by a panel of European vice-presidents using several criteria[2]:

- leadership, teamwork and participation

- customer satisfaction
- process innovation and improvement
- product or service innovation and improvement
- use of data and sound improvement method
- results and measurable business impact.

The rationale is that these awards encourage greater recognition of the efforts people make to create a happy and successful company. The company won an award in the 1991 British Quality Awards for its successful motivation of people for quality excellence.

However, the skill lies in using recognition effectively: too much, and the currency is devalued; too little and individuals feel they have to be superstars. There are also those who say that it can be divisive, but certainly in our culture an individual 'well done' (formal or informal) is a motivator and only the most uncharitable will fail to want to congratulate others for a job well done. At Cyanamid, those chosen are nominated by peers or internal customers and there is a committee monitoring this to check that it is not a mutual admiration society.

Some organizations use particular parts of the workplace to give individuals and groups recognition. For example, Milliken, the textiles manufacturer and recent EFQM award winner, has 'alcoves of excellence', so that there is instant visual impact of quality achievement at strategic points, such as the intersection of corridors. There will be charts showing the progress of projects, teams and individuals involved, with their photographs. The company also has a 'wall of fame' for every area, with plaques, copies of thank you letters or letters of merit with the named individuals involved. All this reinforces the feelings of self-worth. Operators may take visitors on tour, stopping at these points.

The corporate affairs department also has a role here in running features or spotlights on particular sections to ensure maximum exposure of everyone's efforts. BT uses *BT Today*; Milliken, *The Torch*; Royal Mail, *The Courier* and Texaco has a *Quality Newsletter* to enhance awareness of various initiatives.

5.3 CEREMONIES AND CELEBRATION

In order to give wider recognition to individuals through their contribution to their work group, Royal Mail organizes an annual event called

Teamwork. The intention is to show what can be achieved when people are genuinely involved in making improvements to the way they work. The two-day event has an internal focus on colleagues, but certain customers and partners may also be invited.

An exhibition guide is printed with the location of all the stands which are staffed by members of the winning teams. Each stand has a story board with a common format for all the exhibitors: description; participants; project aim; relevant goal; and 'before' and 'after' measurement. The stands are an exercise in creativity, with relevant documentation, equipment and participant games (some computer-based, and some of a 'guess this' type). Staff are eager to show others what they have done and to contact those who may be able to help them. A national improvements database has been compiled of all the projects to make them accessible to all staff, with details of teams so that individuals can contact them. Some projects have found a national application.

This celebration started in 1990 with approximately 45 quality improvement projects. By 1992 there were 100 projects, which has now become the upper limit for the exhibition for logistical reasons. These represented the best projects from the local district teamwork events, which themselves may have selected 25 winners. Some 5000 visitors attend on each of the two days. Around 80 per cent of projects are presented by employees rather than management, and some are in collaboration with large customers. There are no awards; the prize is being there.

Naturally, the event as a whole is assessed for its quality. For example, visitors are asked to rate the quality of projects for content, visual presentation and oral presentation. All the results are then processed so that improvements can be made to the following year's event. Visitors cannot fail to be impressed.

British Gas also has its celebrations and ceremonies for quality. Its 'Gold Flame' award is held at a prestigious hotel in London. The competition is a strong incentive to staff who deal with customers and those who support them. The awards cover a variety of functions: customer accounting, supplies and transport, customer services and engineering. The awards are geared not only to identifying winners and runners up but also the area or function which has shown greatest improvement. This gives recognition to the efforts of a team struggling to improve their business in a depressed area or having to operate with very limited resources. The awards are based on a combination of different criteria. For example, customers' opinions are canvassed, profitability figures are identified, as is the direct cost of providing the essential services.

The competition has been in existence for over 20 years and is a major event in the company calendar. The whole tenor of the event is very professional and guests and participants feel it is an honour to be there. A theme for the occasion is always chosen: one recently selected was the 'Key to Success'. The meaning was twofold: key, as for unlocking a problem or door and key for music so that it can be played in harmony. The compère was a well-known figure in the musical entertainment establishment and the audience was treated to examples of four different types of music: classical; rock, folk and jazz. The message was clear. While the styles varied enormously, they were all playing the same recognizable tune. Just like an organization, the different individuals had different talents and strengths despite their seemingly incompatible styles and dress, yet each was of value to the company. Awards were presented by the chairman and typically received by the most junior member of the team.

British Telecom is another organization which invests much time and effort in ceremony and celebration. Started in 1991, BT has its annual Chairman's Awards for Quality ceremony in BT's London Centre, where those selected receive their own memento and are entertained by board members at a dinner. Team and individual awards are presented where appropriate. At the heart of the success stories is the implementation of the BT values. Of the divisional entries submitted for consideration, only a handful are chosen for the national award; the rest are recognized at their own divisional celebration.

5.4 REWARDS

Research and experience have shown that incentive plans have only been successful in obtaining temporary compliance, so it only appears that gains have been made or problems solved. The negatives of approaching motivation solely in terms of rewards have been succinctly summarized[3] as:

- *Pay, of itself, is not a motivator* (increasing pay does not automatically lead to greater output).
- *Rewards punish* (because they are manipulative and the experience of

being controlled will, over time, become negative; the feeling of exploitation will follow).

- *Rewards rupture relationships* (they reduce the possibilities for cooperation in the scramble for rewards as people pressure the system for individual, non-collective gain; for each person who wins there are losers; staff may conceal problems to be seen as competent by their boss whereas a quality approach requires staff to anticipate and find problems before the customer does).
- *Rewards require reasons for problems and offer the same solution regardless* (pay will improve productivity whereas quality requires that creative solutions are found for problems).
- *Rewards discourage risk taking* (people will do exactly what is asked and no more, no less. No possibilities are explored, no creativity on which continuous improvement relies is shown; predictability and simplicity are sought to get the task done in order to obtain the required reward).
- *Rewards undermine interest* (people do exceptional work because they like what they do; the more we are controlled by rewards the more we lose interest in what we are doing. The interest is in how to get a bonus, not in the quality of the work or the interest of the customers).

While there is much discussion about the effectiveness of rewards (here taken to be money or benefits in kind), most organizations to a greater or lesser extent use these in moderation. There are several types of reward, ranging from cash through to a couple of theatre tickets or a day off. Rewards are often classified into three types:

1 *Individual monetary* (by far the most varied benefits and pay for knowledge, bonuses, suggestions).

2 *Group monetary* (all members of a unit receive a bonus for reaching a predetermined output, gainsharing, profit sharing, stock ownership).

3 *Non-monetary* (discretionary time off, career enhancements, empowerment, recognition).

Each has its own pros and cons, which it is not the purpose to review here.

Incentive gifts of trips abroad used only to be given in sales. But with quality being the responsibility of all (not just those in direct customer contact), there are many deserving people who enable the sales promises to be met. Alternatives have to be found, and firms are looking to team and organizational components to share the rewards. However, team rewards are not without their problems[4]. The two key issues to decide are who is the team and how should it be rewarded. Task forces, partnerships, multi-skilled project teams, product/service work teams, task teams where individuals work to a common goal, all these are different variations. As each team differs in type of membership, stability, objectives and performance measures as well as timescales, it is difficult to reward team performance in the base salary. Rewards tend to come in bonuses tied to strategy or meeting organizational values. Then there is the question of how to deal with exceptional achievement or under-performance in the team (an issue for the team itself to decide?).

The Automobile Association (AA) scheme[5] is called 'Teamwork pays'. Reward is based on elements: organizational performance and local performance measures on which teams compete in leagues, the winners attending an awards ceremony and presentation. The organization-based part is itself divided into quality targets, and financial performance targets. The three national quality targets are:

● number of jobs fixed at the roadside as a percentage of the number undertaken
● average time taken to complete a job from the time the call is taken
● time to respond to a relay call requiring towing away (from request to pick-up).

The system is more detailed than that presented here, but the point is that the quality targets trigger payment in the national financial performance targets. In the second element (team competition) there are seven leagues, covering 180 teams. The teams of 30 people and one supervisor score points monthly against a set of criteria. There are quarterly and annual winners: top of the league and/or which has shown greatest improvement position. Quarterly winners have a team outing from selected options or retail vouchers of up to £100 per person. Patrol team of the year receive a gift and special event, such as a night out for all of them and their families. The organization spends up to £3 million per year on direct incentive awards. What is also expensive is the information back-up required and its communication to the teams to let them know how they are doing.

Increasingly, organization bonuses and individual manager's salaries are being tied to customer satisfaction surveys and other key organizational performance indicators. IBM, Xerox and Royal Mail all do this. Gainsharing, profit sharing and share are other options at this level. For example, IBM has on occasions not awarded any group bonus as the customer satisfaction index was not reached, and Royal Mail ties its divisional management to an agreed target for employee satisfaction, the rationale being that if employees are not satisfied with how they are treated they cannot focus on satisfying the customer.

Competency-based approaches are nearer the ethos of continuous improvement in the learning organization and are increasingly taking over from performance-related pay. Job profiles are created with the associated competences. Jobholders then realize that there is a gap between what they can do and what they are required to do in a new environment which requires transferable skills and flexible attitudes.

At SmithKline Beecham, the international pharmaceutical company, the organization has linked its strategic goals and the executive rewards system. There is one programme worldwide for all the company's executives, and salaries are based on the meeting of nine leadership practices which are abbreviated in Fig. 5.1.

Clearly, these criteria can be individualized within the global system. It can be seen that these mirror very closely the aspects of quality: customer focus, continuous improvement, staff involvement, celebration and personal learning. Many criteria are related to developing people themselves, which is their own reward.

In manufacturing environments, traditional productivity-based

---

- Seeking opportunities to challenge and improve personal performance
- Work with staff individually and as a team to set new targets and the means to achieve them
- Identify and implement improved ways to serve internal and external customers
- Improve SKB's procedures, products and services via quality analysis
- Embrace change for competitive advantage
- Reward and celebrate significant creative achievements
- Develop and appoint high potential people to key positions
- Help all employees achieve their fullest potential by matching their talents with the job
- Communicate openly, honestly and interactively and on a timely basis

---

FIGURE 5.1   Rewarding nine leadership practices in SmithKline Beecham

incentive schemes are not compatible with new manufacturing techniques where emphasis is on speed, flexibility and responsiveness to alterations in customer demand. The need here is to make work more meaningful. It may be that competences related to teamworking and flexibility are the way forward.

5.5 THE APPRAISAL DILEMMA

Appraisal in the traditional sense involves an annual or sometimes six-monthly review of an individual's performance by his or her boss. It is supposed to be a systematic, written procedure endorsed by his or her manager. Typically, performance will be evaluated against the jobholder's key responsibilities and a set of competences and/or other criteria. Appraisal may be seen as having a mixture of different purposes: motivating through objective setting and feedback; rewarding through being tied to pay reviews; or developmental, in being linked to learning and training. Frequently, the aims end up at cross-purposes, or one is over-emphasized at the expense of the other. For example, can there really be open discussion about real weaknesses (rather than cosmetic or allowable ones) when a box rating is going to determine pay? Much has been written about the shortcomings of appraisal, its basic concepts and philosophy, the importance of proper training, forms and procedures. These aspects will not be covered here. The purpose of this section is only to highlight the issues as they relate to quality.

In a quality culture, with its emphasis on continuous improvement and constant and immediate feedback, the appraisal process can seem to be remote and late in the day. A second assumption, that of the centrality of the relationship between individual and boss, does not sit as comfortably in an environment which stresses teamworking and in which an individual may be a member of several groups and have different bosses. How can the individual's contribution be adequately recognized when the boss (by now in a flatter organizational structure and with more reports) is less directly involved in working with the person concerned? Thirdly, the individual normally agrees some performance targets (where the same difficulties of assessing particular contributions would apply). Finally, areas for improvement are highlighted which the individual is expected to pursue, supported by the manager, when perhaps that employee actually needs supporting by the team.

Not surprisingly, companies are beginning to seek out and experiment with new forms. The use of peer feedback is one way of finding out team contribution, although care must be taken to ensure that it is not a method of legitimizing vindictiveness or exerting unfair pressure. Upward feedback on a manager (as at American Express) is becoming more usual, especially for identifying managerial style, and is seen as another innovation in the appraisal process. Royal Mail has done this at all levels, including its front-line staff. Training is offered in giving and receiving feedback, which can be an awesome prospect the first time around. Staff complete forms and send them to a central unit, so the process is anonymous. Managers have to listen to the appraisal on a number of different areas reflecting the leadership charter mentioned in Chapter 1. Criticism must be constructive, and managers will ask: 'What do you want me to do instead?' They have to discuss the findings with their staff and are encouraged to do so with their boss. They then have to devise an action plan and communicate what they are going to do.

The notion of added value in an appraisal is also gaining ground. In determining whether a job is needed, certain questions are likely to be asked:

● What is its special contribution?
● Why is it needed?
● What would happen if the position were eliminated?
● What will change if someone is highly effective in that role?

It is this last point which is particularly relevant to the appraisal process. The individual may achieve economies or be highly efficient or devise new methods which may eliminate a particular task or even the role altogether. Secondly, through teamwork, economies or synergy may evolve. There is also the concept of team added value, which recognizes the contribution made by work flows and the working groups to another area. It may be that it is the performance of a number of tasks by a group during any one time period which becomes the added value, and therefore too narrow a focus on the individual may not be the best assessment of what constitutes added value.

5.6 DISCRETION AND RISK MANAGEMENT

With fewer managerial layers, a set of corporate values espousing customer satisfaction and a mission statement emphasizing quality as a means of staying competitive, an organization is forced to give greater discretion to its employees and manage the consequences of their more direct dealing with customers.

The AA is an organization which has gone down this path. To stay competitive it must not only recruit new members but existing ones. It also has a set of performance measures for customer service and gives verbal assurances for certain categories of breakdown customer that 'someone should be there within the hour'. If for some reason a problem situation develops, patrols, for example, may be empowered to spend £100 and inspectors £300 to compensate a member if they believe this to be necessary. This may take the heat out of a situation and retain the customer in the process. This does not mean that the individual has carte blanche to spend money – these incidents will be monitored and questioned. What it does mean is that no-one will be reprimanded for trying to please the customer in accordance with organizational values.

For this kind of policy to be effective it does require a change in managerial style. Mistakes will occur, over-generous promises may be made to customers and perhaps the organization will be the loser in the short term. What can be done is to constructively take out the learning, see what support may be needed and whether processes have to be changed to ensure that the situation is better structured. It also requires individual managers to be confident in their role, since they are ultimately accountable for their staff's mistakes. It is also a common view among more enlightened management that if people never make mistakes in their work they are probably not being stretched enough.

5.7 SELF-MANAGED WORK GROUPS

Autonomous work groups made their début in this country in the early 1960s, largely as a result of the pioneering work of the Tavistock Institute of Human Relations. These groups were often a means of overcoming the stress and drudgery of mass production or difficult working conditions. Instead of workers being forced to concentrate on minute, repetitive work, the tasks were recombined and they were given more freedom in determining how and when they worked. These ideas were taken further by companies such as Volvo in the manufacture and assembly of their cars and Philips in the assembly work in their TV factories. Gradually these groups took over more and more responsibilities, such as the recruitment and selection of staff and the way in which work should be structured. These kinds of experiments generated all manner of fears in conservative managers: without traditional control over the group, there would be no need for a managerial role and therefore no jobs for them.

More recently, experiments within the Rover Group, the car manufacturer[6] and company well-known for its quality programmes, have led to a team-based organization. Traditionally, managers were spending less than 10 per cent of their time on people issues and the rest driving forward the tasks allocated to their teams. The 'Rover Tomorrow' managers have put this into reverse, spending their time coaching and supporting the team. They have also adopted several responsibilities which were formerly the role of the HR department. The impetus for all these changes came towards the end of the 1980s, when the job of foreman was eliminated, leaving managers with 60 or so direct reports. Team leaders were then introduced who were not part of the management or supervisory structure but worked within the team of 15 to 20 production staff, sometimes elected by team members themselves. The two-day recruitment process (originally developed by personnel to meet legal requirements and company policies) is now carried out by line managers, as is the selection decision and induction process. The team solves its own problems, and few grievances have to be taken through a formal procedure. The propensity towards this form of team depends on the nature of the work: creative and non-routine jobs tend to be more commonly associated with this self-influencing kind of team.

5.8 SELF-MANAGED LEARNING

A related idea which is gaining popularity is that of self-managed learning for staff. In order to properly understand this, it is useful to look first at the broader concept of the learning organization. A definition of a learning organization[7] is: 'one which facilitates the learning of all its members and continually transforms itself'.

Members may include employees, suppliers, customers, governors, neighbours, depending on where the organization wishes to draw the boundaries. There may also be other stakeholders with whom the organization has a close relationship. The concept of transformation is also broad: moving forward, establishing new relations and adopting new technology. The authors provide a set of 11 criteria for a learning organization, and three of these are directly relevant here:

- *intercompany learning* (meeting suppliers or competitors; secondments; benchmarking);
- *a learning climate* (taking the learning out of mistakes; questioning your own practice; admitting you don't know; asking around; valuing continuous improvement);
- *self-development opportunities for all* (opportunities and materials on open access; self-development budgets; exploration of individuals' learning needs; guidance in taking on responsibility; focus on career planning).

Unipart, the supplier of automotive parts, is currently investing £2.5 million in a company university and using its own managers to deliver vocational training to its 3500 employees. The Rover Group has a Masters degree in total quality leadership which it is offering to its managers in collaboration with Liverpool John Moores University. This will be of benefit to the organization not only through bringing in new skills and knowledge but in the tackling of a major business change project over a six-month period. In a similar vein, Lloyds Bank has 132 multimedia open learning centres where some 20 core training courses can be accessed voluntarily.

Self-managed learning (SML) can occur either individually or in groups. In the former case it is completely self-directed and, as such, may not benefit from the support and experience of being part of a group. In the latter case, SML is about individuals working in a small group to set job-related learning objectives. The group is there to help individuals to clarify and achieve these objectives; in some cases members may be able to supply contacts and resources to do this. Its particular value is that, as most training and development is line-directed, it provides a scheme which is employee-centred and directed. People may join who are within the same function but from different parts of the organization, or they may share a common interest in a particular problem. There are no hard and fast rules.

What does seem to matter is to have some clear, broad, ground rules at the start so that groups can evolve their own process. Certainly there is a form and a language to be learned for working in these groups, sharing information and handling conflict. That is why they work better when they have access to a facilitator who can help with the diagnosis and articulation of concerns, and the development of a way of working with which all feel comfortable.

Organizationally, there needs to be a framework to hold together the network of groups as they form and disband. Agreements need to be made with line managers in terms of release, attendance and what, if any, resources they are prepared to provide. They, in turn, need to be assured that there are benefits relevant to both the individual and the organization. It certainly offers staff a way to work on the results of performance appraisal which, in turn, is there to support the business. It should also make an organization a more attractive place to work, since it increases support via networking and the organization makes a small budget available to them to signal its commitment.

SML groups may fail to develop for a number of reasons: members may have jobs which entail a high degree of travelling and cannot make their regular appointments; groups may have one member who is in a line reporting relationship; they may be composed of people who are not used to peer teamwork; or some may not properly define their learning objectives.

5.9 RECRUITMENT AND SELECTION POLICIES AND PROCESSES

With different kinds of values, new organization structures with an emphasis on faster responses and use of technology and teamworking, what approach needs to be taken in finding suitable people for the work? The director of personnel and information systems at Nissan UK, Peter Wickens, has gone on record as saying:

> It is critical that we in the manufacturing industry realize that the first line supervisor, if carefully selected, highly motivated and given the appropriate status, can make more difference to the long-term success of the company than any other group other than top management. And even here, it is the supervisors who deliver the top management policies.

The point made here is that careful recruitment and selection is important, as supervisors in a quality-oriented company will be called upon to do much more than in the past: problem solving, team building, coaching, and understanding data and converting them into information on which action can be taken. All this is vital for a quality company. The era of the graduate supervisor has already arrived.

The retail trade has always had a reputation for high turnover of staff and poor morale. Safeway, the giant grocery chain, has been involved with a major supplier of psychometrics and other instruments in a project to completely change the way in which they recruit all their staff below supervisor level. The rationale given was that it wanted to gain competitive advantage by recruiting people who were likely to be better at serving the customer.

Recruitment and selection are important not only to secure the correct people but also to ensure that they are likely to stay. Professional services businesses, such as insurance, rely in the main on good face-to-face communication and telephone skills. Aspects such as financial competence and continuity of contact are vital in retaining business. Yet it has been reported[8] that almost 80 per cent of life insurance salespeople leave their companies within two years of joining. The various surveys reported highlight a poorly managed industry. Those with larger sales forces (700 or more) tended to have better retention rates. However, with each salesperson costing over £10,000 to recruit, it is not in the industry's best interests to let this situation continue. Over-selling and misselling will obviously damage credibility and any image of quality.

5.10 EMPLOYMENT POLICIES AND PRACTICES

Developing a quality company may often require a shift from traditional ways of working. As organizations are increasingly required to deliver their services faster and be more accessible, while controlling their costs, they may need to reappraise their ways of working. In the annual hours system, staff are contracted to work on an annual basis, thus allowing employers to have flexibility in the scheduling of their work. Matsushita Electronics in Cardiff, which manufactures colour televisions and microwaves, has introduced annual hours[9] to overcome the seasonal variation in demand for electrical goods, with almost two-thirds being required between September and December. This enabled the organization to reorganize the staff's available hours over the year to reduce stocks and boost production to meet customer demands. This has reduced the costs in peak season recruitment and overtime. Other organizations known to be using this system are Welsh Water, Rockware Glass, ITN and Bristol and West Building Society. The reported gains are:

- cost savings and reduced overtime
- improved productivity and extended operating hours
- more flexibility and better teamworking
- reduced absenteeism and improved motivation and morale
- higher guaranteed earnings for employees and more time off
- greater predictability.

These interact and benefit both the employees and the organization.

5.11 COMMUNICATIONS

Within a quality-oriented company, communications have to be timely and comprehensive. At a strategic level, top management has to be more open about the business to show employees how quality is impacting on the bottom line. At an operational level, defining what quality is for all employees and making sure that everyone understands how a quality philosophy affects them and what contribution they themselves make to it are key messages to impart. Communication is also an important way of securing and maintaining commitment to quality throughout the organization.

It is not the purpose here to give an overview of communication theory and practice, and in any case one particular method – employee surveys – will be covered later in the chapter. However, the way in which change is communicated to staff will affect the support and commitment which ensue. Managers know that they must decide on the most appropriate objectives, the 'audience', the channels they want to use and the feedback loops they wish to tap to ensure that the message has been received. What needs to be stressed is that good communication is essential for any quality initiative as it keeps staff informed, ensures understanding and enables people to work together.

There are a number of issues which need to be carefully considered. Advanced disclosure can generate anxiety, since many questions may be raised which either have not been thought through or to which there are no satisfactory answers. There is also likely to be intense political activity while people try to position themselves to take advantage of the situation. The consultative process is useful in taking people along with the change, but it is also time-consuming and can slow down the momentum for the change.

Typically, organizations use a number of different channels. In times of upheaval, especially in larger organizations, there is a need to reinforce the reasons for change, the new culture and values and the role of quality. Royal Mail, for example, used a video of its CEO to do this. The corporate newsletter is another medium. British Telecom, British Airways and Texaco use this to inform staff of successes, corporate events and competitions relating to quality. They also use it to report new initiatives or systems to support customers and areas of the organization's successful collaboration with suppliers and customers. British Telecom uses its newsletter to announce that its 'high-quality service' has won contracts in manufacturing, food and construction. The quality message is also reinforced by wallcharts covering mission and values and the appropriate standards of behaviour expected. Very often firms will employ an outside group of consultants to customize a series of handbooks to convey the quality message. British Gas (North Thames Ltd) did this in an excellent handbook entitled *Total Quality and You*, which aimed to explain what total quality was and how it was relevant to the individual in the workplace. The booklet anchored quality in a business philosophy, why it was crucial, its principles, and the importance of the customers and teamwork. This it did in a jargon-free, direct way. There are also related booklets on problem solving, project management and associated tools and techniques. Departmental events such as team awards (see section 3) are another way of spreading the word, as are line managers briefing their staff and those working in cross-functional teams.

If there is one key quality message which needs to be communicated, it is the requirement for setting high standards and ensuring that these are met. This should not be a one-way flow. Sometimes senior management needs exposure to feed back both positive and negative aspects, and this can be done in a variety of ways, for example, live question and answer sessions or highlights from these reported in newsletters (as in the case of BT). Focus groups (see Chapter 3) provide another valuable means to glean feedback.

Workshops are yet another way of spreading the word. As part of a cultural transformation, Air Products communicated the launch of TQM with quality awareness workshops[10]. These were to introduce the concept of TQM and were designed to be highly participative. They began with top management and cascaded down the organization so that a critical mass of people were trained, thus increasing the chances that they would be committed to quality. This awareness phase took two years to complete.

Realizing the difficulties associated with any change, Royal Mail has introduced a change code which relies on a good communications strategy. The code ensures that employees will be informed of changes in working practices or locations well in advance of when they are due to occur. The code has been endorsed by both the Communications Managers Association and the Union of Communication Workers.

5.12 STAFF SURVEYS

A special form of communication is staff surveys. They are becoming increasingly common as organizations seek to maximize employee satisfaction in order to deliver a high-quality service. Keeping in touch is especially important in times of change. Reports of surveys carried out at the BBC and British Airways[11] suggest that, despite great pride in being part of such organizations, employees felt that they were being let down by management at all levels. It is noteworthy that both these organizations are regarded as providing a quality service by the general public, and it shows the importance of not taking the attitudes of those staff who deliver the service for granted. For example, staff at the BBC felt insecure and uninvolved, and the corporation was trying to tackle this by encouraging more open discussion.

The BA survey 'Input '93' showed that only 39 per cent said that they were well or fairly well managed and 33 per cent said that managers were good at giving honest feedback, managing change, listening, delegating or recognizing effort. On open-ended questions, the most frequently mentioned subject was management. British Airways' reaction was to say that it wanted to prove that it was prepared to act on the findings, otherwise the credibility of any future surveys would suffer. A similar reaction was taken by the BBC, who asked all employees to discuss the survey findings with their managers.

British Telecom has a CARE survey (Communications and Attitude Research for Employees). In 1993, more than 125 000 BT people (75 per cent of the workforce) responded. The group managing director, Michael Hepher, was reported as saying that the management team spent a great deal of time going over the results. He said that in future actions needed to be labelled as resulting specifically from the CARE survey so that employees knew that their views were drawing a response from the company. A year later, there was found to be a marked improvement in many of the areas. Of 69 result areas, 54 improved, 12 deteriorated and three remained unchanged.

Royal Mail carries out its staff survey at quarterly intervals so that all its staff are covered annually. At divisional level, the management team is judged on whether certain targets of employee satisfaction have been reached. Some may have started from a low base with an aim to raise it gradually by a few per cent. If they meet these targets they are given a bonus. If there is a difficult change ahead, they are forced to give it more time so that the satisfaction rating does not drop. As with all such techniques of corporate communication, the caveat is to avoid possible defensive reasoning which encourages staff to believe that their role is to criticize management, who are then supposed to 'fix' things. This attitude could discourage people from examining their own behaviour and taking some responsibility for the situation.

5.13 TRAINING FOR QUALITY

Although the process of communication, surveys and training has been split up for the purposes of analysis, it will by now be evident that not only do they all reinforce each other in conveying the quality message, but the distinction between them in their application tends to blur. Royal Mail combines the two and speaks of training and communication. Its process involved five-day workshops for all senior and middle managers and cascaded down in work teams. Therefore there was also a double involvement of many managers, both as participant and as team leader. For first line managers, training was via workshops or in modules. In the case of operational employees, there were communications and awareness sessions as well as skill training linked to improvement activities.

In a quality-focused organization, training is seen as an investment, not a cost, and, as such, is always high on the managerial agenda. At Corning Glass, the strategy is to train all employees, the goal being for each one to spend 5 per cent of his or her working time in education and training. Corning employees are used as instructors, as it was felt that they would be more credible than outsiders. Typically, the training will take place immediately a new quality initiative has been announced and at all Corning locations affected worldwide. Training is mandatory, which shows employees the depth of commitment in the company.

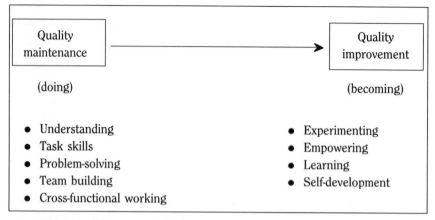

FIGURE 5.2   Training and development for quality

Source: F.A. Clark, 'Public Awareness'. Reproduced with permission from the *Total Quality Management Magazine*, December 1992

The content of training for quality typically starts with awareness training (reasons, principles, values); workshops on what quality means for me and my job; customer orientation; leadership, management, teamwork and problem solving. Once these basics have been put in place, which usually takes the best part of 18 months, new initiatives may be spun off requiring different forms of training. All this enables the organization to attain the required base level of quality and maintain it[12]. However, training in these task-based skills is rarely enough to meet the challenge of continuous improvement. A diagram of the author's which may help to explain this is shown in Fig. 5.2.

Because of pressures from the environment, the requirement is always to improve even further. This needs a change in attitudes and culture to enable staff to be empowered to take decisions, learn from controlled experiments where relevant and develop themselves in the meantime. The change which is necessary is from 'doing better' to 'becoming better'. If this does not occur, how can staff respond to the constant and new challenges which face them?

An example of a professional approach to training is Royal Mail's 'Customer First' programme. To begin with, employees were shown a video on the subject and encouraged to work on teamwork charts to identify who their customers were and their requirements, their suppliers, and any quality improvements identified by the individual. There was also a briefing booklet available about the total quality process at Royal Mail. A glossy workbook (Part 3 of the programme) summarized what had gone before and encouraged individuals to:

- understand why their personal involvement was essential to Royal Mail and Customer First
- identify how the business mission and values directly affected them
- enable them to put forward their best quality idea.

Helped by quality facilitators, employees worked their way through this self-completion booklet.

What was particularly helpful was the visual impact and layout of the pages. Questions were asked, an example answer given to start off the thinking process and a list of what other Royal Mail employees had said (not always complimentary!) to root out the problems by encouraging employees to be constructively critical. The training did not allow the employee to be passive. The output of the workbook was a quality improvement idea which, if they wanted to take it forward, they could do so with assistance and information about commitment. Employees thus had an attractive record of what the programme meant and their own ideas towards it in a reference document.

British Telecom has also undertaken massive quality-related training. Two key programmes at the end of 1993 were Leading through Teamwork and Involving Everyone. Some 30 000 managers took part in the first programme. More than 1300 two-and-a-half-day leadership courses were held at 12 venues and involved some 1000 event managers. One important aspect was to monitor the outcomes, and the top personal learning points extracted were:

- the value of others' criticisms
- the effect of giving and receiving feedback
- the importance of planning
- listening to others
- time management.

The second initiative, 'Involving Everyone', was for BT's 140 000 non-managers. More than 11 000 teams attended the one-day introductory session dealing with total quality principles, teamwork and the commercial realities facing BT. The follow-up sessions held in the workplace covered each team's customers, suppliers, activities, quality measurement and continuous improvement. The teams then set up quality improvement projects to put the lessons learned into practice.

5.14 CONCLUSION

The policies and processes described here do not act in isolation and all have a vital part to play in making quality live within the organization. Ten years ago, most of these would have been seen as the main responsibility of the HR department acting as a facilitator and provider of guidelines and best practice. Now they have become the concern of line managers in an active dialogue with HR.

ACTION QUESTIONS

- What recognition and rewards are there in your organization for emphasizing the importance of quality?
- Are there clear policies regarding appraisal, employment and communications and how do they contribute to achieving quality? Are they checked via staff surveys?
- What is your organization doing to encourage self-managed learning as part of the overall effort for continuous improvement?

REFERENCES

1 IPM (1993): *People Management Matters*, IPM, Wimbledon, UK.

2 Atkinson, R. (1992): 'Motivating People for Success', *Total Quality Management*, August, pp. 251-3.

3 Kohn, A. (1993): 'Why Incentive Plans Cannot Work', *Harvard Business Review*, September/October, pp. 54-63.

4 Murlis, H. (1994): 'The Challenge of Rewarding Teamwork', *Personnel Management*, February, p. 8.

5 Pickard, J. (1993): 'How Incentives Can Drive Teamworking', *Personnel Management*, September, pp. 26-32.

6 Arthur, M. (1994): 'Rover Managers Learn to take a Back Seat', *Personnel Management*, October, pp. 58-63.

7 Pedler, M., Burgoyne, J. and Boydell, T. (1991): *The Learning Company: A Strategy for Sustainable Development*, McGraw-Hill, Maidenhead, UK.

8 Nuki, P. (1993): 'Short Life for Policies Sold by Itinerant Salesmen', *Sunday Times* Personal Finance, Section 4, p. 1.

9 Hutchinson, S. (1994): 'The Changing Face of Annual Labour', *Personnel Management*, April, pp. 42-7.

10 Atkinson, R. (1992): 'Motivating People for Success', *Total Quality Management*, August, pp. 251-3.

11 PM News (1993): *Personnel Management*, August, p. 5.

12 Clark, F.A. (1992): 'Public Awareness', *Total Quality Management Magazine*, December, pp. 373-8.

The role of the leader: facing out

6.1 INTRODUCTION

One of the key reasons why organizations adopt quality is that they believe it will offer competitive advantage. However, this will not happen unless the message reaches the various stakeholders in the outside world: customers, suppliers, investors, regulators and the general public.

6.2 COMMUNICATING THE QUALITY STRATEGY TO CUSTOMERS

There are many ways of communicating the quality strategy to customers, both implicit and explicit. Organizations may categorize their customers according to size and requirements and tailor their services accordingly, showing a more targeted approach to quality. For example, BT has its global customer service team, which was restructured to give a clearer focus on different types of business. The first group is the top 50, who have dedicated service managers, possessing a deep knowledge of customers' needs, and providing high levels of service anywhere in the world. A second tier of 350 are looked after by service centres in the UK and by multifunctional teams specializing in certain business sectors. A third group of 1200 medium-sized business customers receive dedicated support. This organization reflects a move away from the all-purpose, geographical organization to one dedicated to segments of the business world.

Responsiveness to crises and the unexpected is also another way of showing the outside world by actions how organizations are geared to meeting customer needs at short notice. For example, half an hour after an explosion in the City of London, the BT staff were in touch with customers and repair teams were on various sites soon afterwards.

Another way of demonstrating the quality strategy externally is by involving customers in the design of new products or services through joint projects to find out what they want and need. In fact, Digital Equipment found to its cost that often a constructive strategy foundered because it was poorly communicated to customers. Sometimes customers felt that they were being offloaded to resellers to cut the company's sales costs.

The design of special centres to cater for customers, discuss their business needs and with enough flexibility to configure various pieces of equipment or aspects of service is another way of communicating the quality strategy. British Telecom has designed such a centre, which depends on teams gathering information about customers' business needs in advance and providing a flexible environment with innovative, business-focused demonstrations. The layout has a reception area, auditorium, display area and core room for discussion, using infloor wiring to give maximum flexibility for positioning displays and demonstrations. A central presentation system, using a multimedia approach, can be programmed for individual visits. Computer-controlled illumination can precede visitors around the centre, highlighting particular areas.

There may also be merit in auditing the channels of external communication to customers to see how effectively they are being used to publicize a quality strategy. This can be done through consulting user groups, trade associations and monitoring reactions in the industrial or sectoral press. All of these are very quick to publicize poor quality without much prompting; however, they often need to be positively encouraged to report good practice.

British Telecom tries to get close to the customer by holding quality seminars for its clients to show them what initiatives are going on internally. They may have a talk on BT's quality strategy and be given insights into particular quality initiatives or be asked to participate in special interactive exercises to increase their awareness of BT's quality activities.

The secondary education sector (especially the independent one) is adept at this form of customer relations, with its numerous open days, concerts, publicity in the local community and the calling of influential figures to serve on the board of governors. One recent communication from a local school which I came across was: 'XYZ school, here to serve the community through the pursuit of excellence'.

There was a charter, beginning with 'Every parent has the right to expect...', with ten detailed points made about the services. What was striking was that the succinct and strong style was more reminiscent of a commercial operation than what would traditionally be expected of a local school.

6.3 COMMUNICATING THE QUALITY STRATEGY TO SUPPLIERS

Perhaps one of the most powerful communications that an organization takes quality very seriously is the care it invests in supplier selection and management. Those who have policies which are stringent and are designed to prevent degradation through swift and firm action are likely to discourage the marginal performers or those who are not interested in continuous improvement themselves.

The reactive role is for purchasing or other functions to have regular reports on any failures or problems traceable to the supplier so that immediate action may be taken. This may then involve their close collaboration in the discussion of findings of investigations of problems and the setting of new goals for supplier quality.

The proactive role is to involve suppliers at the start of new product or service initiatives so that they can gear up internally to meet the change in requirements. Invitations to attend design reviews and presentations on new customer demands ensure that things are done with suitable lead times and to the satisfaction of both parties.

An interesting example of collaboration is seen in BP Exploration's deal with three computer services suppliers[1], with payment linked to the level of savings achieved. The 'high risk, high reward deals' with SEMA, Syncordia and Saic involved the contracting out of IT staff, hardware and help desks. British Petroleum's view was that the higher the savings, the greater were their profits, assuming that the quality of service was maintained. If savings fell below a minimum level, the suppliers would make a loss. British Petroleum and its suppliers have an 'open book' arrangement, where they have to show each other their financial accounts relating to the arrangement.

In the case of professional services, requirements of the supplier may be that several aspects of the process are assessed: the actual delivery of services and their assessment; the various processes undertaken to monitor and manage internal quality; and guaranteeing that the people who are to deliver the services are capable and competent to do so.

A successful relationship between companies has been said to rely on eight Is[2]:

1 *Individual excellence* (positive motives, looking for opportunities rather than masking weaknesses).
2 *Importance* (strategic importance of relationship crucial to long-term goal).
3 *Interdependence* (neither can 'go it alone').
4 *Investment* (devote financial and other resources to the relationship).
5 *Information* (share the information required to make the relationship work).
6 *Integration* (shared ways of operating smoothly; connections between many people at different levels needed).
7 *Institutionalization* (relationship given a formal status with clear responsibilities and decisions).
8 *Integrity* (behave towards each other in an honourable way in order to develop trust).

If all these things apply between supplier and customer, then that is the strongest indication that the customer is communicating successfully its quality strategy and requirements. To make this work requires leadership at all levels to cement the relationship critical to smooth delivery.

6.4 NETWORKING WITH STAKEHOLDERS

Apart from the customers and suppliers, one of the key aspects in keeping an organization successful is its relationship with various stakeholders. The leaders, especially those at the top of the organization, will have the responsibility of safeguarding the corporate image and explaining their policies and actions to the outside world. In an environment increasingly characterized by complex relationships (which can also be affected very quickly by rumour as well as fact), it is important to know the currency of information and to be able to influence and react to it.

Non-executive directors (see Chapter 2) are helpful here in

communicating quality strategy and policy and offering reassurance about how the organization is handling its affairs in relation to its shareholders and the general public. They may also be crucial in helping to obtain resources for the organization and obtaining access to quality-related issues such as competitor benchmarking.

Shareholders also need to be informed of the organization's quality strategy, since it is linked to competitive edge and profitability (Chapter 2) and will therefore affect the share price and hence the return on their investment.

The media and the professional and trade press can also be positively influenced. This can be done by encouraging them to report case histories or new initiatives in the quality field that organizations are undertaking. These examples then have a spin-off effect as they become regarded as best practice and are thus a secondary source of advertising.

6.5 CHECKING CUSTOMERS' PERCEPTIONS

One of the dangers of only communicating to customers that there is a policy and strategy for quality is that it may not actually be perceived to operate. That is why leaders need to closely monitor their customers' perceptions, ensure that the processes for doing so are accurate and that action is taken on the results.

Corning Glass has become known for its close ties between its quality drives and customer requirements[3]. For example, in one operation, certain staff regularly met customers to check that the specifications used were realistic. They wished to avoid demanding excessively rigorous tolerances on dimensions which were not critical to product performance. Instances were cited of Corning's production workers corresponding directly with production workers at customers' premises to see that their needs were being met.

In their internal newsletter, BT quoted a survey of what customers were likely to expect from them towards the end of the decade[4], although it felt that, in practice, they expected these characteristics of a quality organization now:

- commitments made by individuals have to be kept by the organization
- to be known and respected, with a named contact
- to be in control of the relationship

- to be listened to and understood as individuals
- fast response and consistent quality
- 'no break' service culture and access to the right person or system
- access to the latest technology.

6.6 CHECKING SUPPLIERS' PERCEPTIONS

Suppliers themselves have power in the marketplace (see Chapter 2) if they themselves have few competitors or supply something which is highly valued by the customer. That is why it becomes crucial for leaders in an organization to manage suppliers' perceptions of how important they are to their quality strategy in a realistic and balanced way. If undue importance is given to their demands, the quality/price ratio of an organization's products and services will suffer. If too little attention is paid, suppliers will feel undervalued and uncommitted to an organization's plans. They will comply as long as they have to do so. The classic case is that of a supplier of a large food or retail chain who feels that unfair advantage has been taken by its customer by offering to take volume (equivalent to security) in exchange for lower prices. In reality, the chain can switch suddenly, leaving its suppliers extremely vulnerable if their organizations have been specifically geared up to meet its needs.

One way of avoiding these imbalances is to adopt a collaborative supplier/user model rather than a controller/giver relationship. This model encourages close collaboration in terms of the design and provision of a product or service so that suppliers can effect their own internal changes with a suitable lead time and enable training and development of staff to take place where appropriate as well as make any necessary changes in policies, processes or technology.

6.7 LIAISING WITH CENTRES OF EXCELLENCE

One of the roles of the leader in such an empirically-driven discipline is to keep in touch with centres of excellence to see what is being done in the quality field and identify any problems associated with approaches, tools and techniques and consultants. There are a number of different sources which can be contacted in order to keep up to date. These sources have different roles, which will affect what they can offer. Accreditation bodies such as the British Standards Institute will be able to give specific guidance on their required procedures and may often have industry or sector specialists to guide an organization through their application procedure.

Another category acts more like brokers of knowledge and education and adopts a role of bringing interested parties together in various collaborative ventures. The European Foundation for Quality Management (EFQM), apart from its awarding role, encourages the undertaking of research into quality. It also has service focus groups which convene to tackle particular issues and runs a publications business. The British Quality Association (whose aim is to promote the best practice in quality management within the UK) has a similar remit, and recognizes benchmarking as an important tool, organizing seminars around this topic.

The original gurus such as Deming, Juran and Crosby have their own institutes and consultancies to publicize their own approaches. They provide training and their own materials for education in quality management. As such, they may be useful in promoting reference sites, but cannot be considered independent in the advice they offer.

Business schools and polytechnics often have units or groups of staff and postgraduate students working in the field. They are able to offer advice, in-depth research and may undertake consultancy for accreditation purposes and for other bodies, professional institutes or brokers in the quality field. Their advantage is that they are independent and can offer expert advice in methodologies.

6.8 BENCHMARKING

Apart from liaising with centres of excellence, benchmarking is another way in which leaders can find out what is happening. Its aim is to focus the organization on the best way of carrying out its operations and anticipating future needs to ensure superior performance. Comparisons of each of the key activities are made by the best practitioner that one can find. The process has been comprehensively reviewed elsewhere[5], but there are several key points which are important. Benchmarking is essentially about measuring the organization against external criteria and translating the information back into the organizational business and quality strategies.

The main types of benchmarking are set out below, and their use will depend on what the organization's objectives are:

- *internal* (against similar units in a large organization such as a health authority or multinational. It is relatively easy to do since data and other information are more easily available and in a similar format. Access and confidentiality are less of a problem, but the information will not be 'best in class');
- *competitive* (this will provide a standard, but will be more difficult to obtain if it is the basis of competitive advantage);
- *functional* (functional excellence is compared within a sector);
- *generic* (processes which are common across all organizations are compared such as invoicing systems. This is easier to do since they are probably not the basis of reputation or advantage).

The process of benchmarking widens company horizons. Restricting comparisons to similar businesses in similar markets and situations will not lead to significant breakthroughs which could overcome particular assumptions within the sector. In fact, there can be no limit to the search for best practice. The more creative the thinking, the better. For example, Xerox compared its distribution against 3M in Düsseldorf, Ford in Cologne, a Sainsbury's regional depot, a Volvo parts distribution centre, a warehouse in Gothenburg and IBM's French warehouse.

Many companies have gone on record as undertaking benchmarking – Unilever, AT&T, ICL, Sears Plc, Guinness and Royal Doulton. In general, the process involves knowing the difference, from a customer's viewpoint, between an ordinary and an extraordinary supplier and setting standards for this. It means understanding what the best organizations do to achieve them and applying the experience in a critical, sensitive way. The key is modifying and translating the findings from other environments, yet making due allowance for cultural differences. The gap between the actual and desired performance is identified, and likely future performance levels are projected against it.

A critical question is actually deciding what to benchmark and at what degree of detail. It requires a focus (an organization cannot benchmark everything at once). Elements in the strategy or areas which are detracting from an organization's performance will generate ideas. In particular, by getting close to the customer and using all the feedback obtained (see Chapter 3) organizations should be able to determine what changes would lead to improved relationships with the customer, make an impact on profitability or generate innovation. Key processes may be supply chain management, financial control, billing or customer service delivery, to name but a few.

Selecting a partner will depend not only on the area of interest but also on the type of benchmarking mentioned earlier in this chapter. There are several sources (see section 6). Customers may well have very strong views about who they think is excellent in a particular area. The sectoral press will also generate ideas. In selecting the partner (assuming that the relevance criteria have been met), a useful guideline might be whether, if they came and asked to look around our organization we would be able to give them the information we are asking them for. This is important, as the process is not about industrial spying and there may be certain types of information exchange which may be precluded by UK, European or other countries' legal systems.

Obtaining the information is probably easier than first appears. The different sources of information from centres of excellence, trade associations, databases, customers and suppliers, market research and customer service units will all yield leads and insights. However, personal contact and site visits are the only way to understand how an organization achieves superior performance.

Preparation for the visit is essential. That means sifting through everything that has been gleaned so far and concentrating on supplementing it or asking only for the information necessary to make a direct comparison of performance. It is also important to think how the relevant information might be quantified and what infrastructure needs to be in place to support it. Several practices can contribute to the gap in actual and desired performance: methods underlying the process itself; business practices surrounding it; the allocation of resources and the operational structure.

It is also important to decide on the relevant people to make the visit. At the very least, there should be a technical or functional expert on the process in question and someone senior enough to help ensure that any good ideas or changes arising from the benchmarking exercise will have a realistic chance of being implemented. Ideally, more should go to ensure that there is a critical mass of people who can support any changes recommended.

Benchmarking is not a quick fix. A benchmarking project may take up to six months. Naturally, close relationships are made during this time and will tend to be maintained for later visits. Groups will tend to form and take on the nature of a select club to share their information as mutual trust grows. This can make it difficult for a new organization to 'break in' later on.

Benchmarking is a learning process and there are naturally pitfalls to avoid. The first is that it should not be seen as industrial tourism, with expense accounts for everyone to have time out or trips abroad. The visits may be interpreted as some kind of 'gold rush' to pick the brains of the best and make a fortune. Not surprisingly, without thorough preparation and an intention to lift ideas and apply them directly, the results of such visits will quickly fall into disrepute. Another problem which can ruin the process is analysis and measurement paralysis. Above all, the findings must be translated into action plans to improve the existing processes, using a sound rationale.

Sometimes benchmarking may fail because the wrong measure has been chosen due to inadequate knowledge of the organization as a result of poor preliminary research. Not setting aside enough time or resources is another reason for failure or being over-ambitious in the number of things to benchmark. Over- or under-selling is a further aspect to be avoided. The main way to prevent all this is to ensure that benchmarking is linked into the business plan. If this is done, many of these reasons for failure will fall away.

The benefits of benchmarking are necessarily being recognized by senior managers as a powerful tool to provide the stimulus and knowledge to make changes to improve business performance. They are:
- encouraging innovation in business processes
- providing new momentum for total quality processes
- setting demanding but realistic performance targets
- guiding investments
- reducing spending in non-strategic costs
- motivating people by showing what can be done
- creating a receptive attitude to change
- providing support for the internal champion.

The true benefit lies in continual recalibrating to keep up to date with changing business conditions, and the technique is becoming accepted in the UK (BT, British Steel, ICL and Shell do this). In the UK, the British Quality Foundation promotes benchmarking and the DTI Enterprise

Initiative regards it as an important topic within the wider subject of performance measurement. The EFQM model also presupposes benchmarking against 'best in class'. In conclusion, benchmarking does make people observe and creatively adapt best practices. It also has a motivational effect because it shows what can be done elsewhere, creating a receptive attitude where there might otherwise have been collective deafness to the words of an internal 'champion'.

6.9 WHAT KIND OF ACCREDITATION?

Part of the leader's role is to be sensitive to the external image of the organization. In some industries, notably manufacturing and engineering, customers are demanding that their suppliers show some form of minimum guaranteed quality such as BS5750 or ISO 9000. In fact, these may be a licence to do business, and failure to display the quality 'kitemark' may mean a loss of exports. However, these forms of accreditation are not themselves guarantees of quality, and some organizations fear that they generate a compliance mentality which may cut across the broader quality philosophy which the organizations are trying to generate. That is to say, the idea of annual external audits and inspectors may lead to a sense of achieving only the routine.

There is a vast array of organizations which have the British Standards approval: hospital trusts, training organizations, consultants, financial advisers, the police, as well as the more traditional manufacturing plants. However, organizations may well acquire several accreditations at once. For example, the leader may well be faced with a decision whether to work towards the Investors in People (IIP) award or his or her own industry's charter.

The IIP award is often seen as complementary to the BS5750 award. This is because it focuses on the contribution of people management to the overall business mission and strategy, covering all aspects from recruitment to development of staff and communications. It is seen as a way of humanizing the 'systems' focus of BS5750 and highlighting the importance of the way people are managed for delivering a high-quality service. The award has four national standards, each accompanied by several indicators which arise directly from it (in total, 24 which an organization has to meet).

Organizations in the public sector have their own charters. In January

1992, the British prime minister announced details of the Chartermark Quality Award. Its aim is to recognize those who achieve most against the Citizen's Charter principles. The government identified six principles of public service, given below in shortened form:

1 *Standards* (explicit, monitored and published).

2 *Information and openness* (full, accurate information about the service, costs and performance).

3 *Choice and consultation* (users help to set priorities).

4 *Courtesy and helpfulness* (staff to be identifiable to the customer, service to suit convenience of the customer, customer service policy in place).

5 *Putting things right* (effective complaints procedure and swift and effective remedy).

6 *Value for money* (effective and efficient use of taxpayers' money).

These six are the qualifying criteria. The winners were to demonstrate, in addition, measurable improvements in quality of service, increased customer satisfaction, and plans for innovation to the service or at least one enhancement at no extra cost to the taxpayer. Job Centres, London Underground, the Department of Social Security, the Law Courts and Customs and Excise are illustrative of the organizations covered. Most have their own charters, such as the National Health Service with its Patient's Charter. However, a government-sponsored survey[6] of more than 3000 people conducted a year and a half after the initiative showed that it was not delivering the hoped-for results. In fact, most believed that standards in the then British Rail, the National Health Service, council housing, the police service and roads had either shown no improvement or had declined.

The situation of the Citizen's Charter illustrates the importance of the careful use of these awards in being managed in the context of customer and supplier perceptions (see earlier). It also shows the importance of not raising expectations without being confident of the ability to deliver and ensuring that results are communicated to the relevant stakeholders. Other accreditation awards will be mentioned in more detail in subsequent sections. These encompass broader areas than those such as BS5750 and IIP.

6.10 EUROPEAN AWARDS

The European Foundation for Quality Management (EFQM) was set up in 1988 by 14 leading Western European companies in acknowledgement of the key role that quality plays in the delivery of competitive advantage. By 1994 membership had grown to more than 370 organizations covering most European countries and sectors. The prizes and awards for quality are based on the following model (Fig. 6.1). There are nine elements to the model which are used as criteria against which an organization's progress towards quality can be measured. The criteria are divided into two groups: *results* (what the organization has and is achieving); and *enablers* (the factors determining how the results are achieved). The logic is that customer satisfaction, people (employee) satisfaction, and impact on society are achieved through leadership driving policy and strategy, people management and processes.

The model is based on the notion of self-appraisal (each of the criteria carries a certain percentage of the total points). Organizations are able to assess their current position, identify their strengths and weaknesses and work out an improvement plan. When they feel sufficiently confident of obtaining a prize, they prepare for an external assessment. This is usually preceded by their own staff attending a training programme so that they can advise on areas to be developed and on how to present a case.

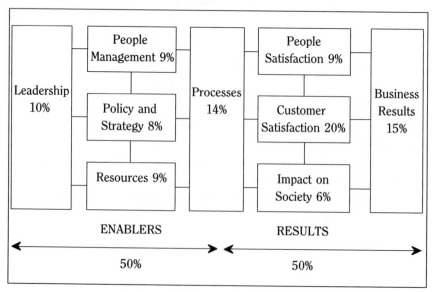

FIGURE 6.1   The EFQM model

Assessors for the awards and prizes are usually drawn from organizations which do not have any vested interests in the results. From the assessment, further points are awarded for improvement and an opportunity to go for the European Quality Award, awarded to the most successful exponent of total quality. Milliken's European Division, with its headquarters in the north-west of England, won the 1993 award. It is a subsidiary of the US organization which had already won the Malcolm Baldridge National Quality Award in 1989. The company manufactures textile products (from carpets to the covering for tennis balls). The previous year it had come second; yet that year's report contained more than 80 specific recommendations for potential improvement. Milliken had worked on its pursuit of excellence process for 13 years. All this gives some idea of how difficult it is to obtain an award. The managing director, Clive Jeanes, summed up the process:

> It's a bit like climbing a mountain and seeing the challenge of the next ridge stretching off into the distance .... I would guess that if there is a destination for total quality, then we are no more than 25 per cent or 30 per cent on the way towards it.

6.11 AMERICAN AND JAPANESE AWARDS

The Malcolm Baldridge National Quality Award is an annual event to recognize US companies which excel in quality achievement and quality management. The guidelines describe the award processes and requirements and provide a basis for self-assessment for organizations pursuing quality excellence.

There are seven examination categories (with fuller descriptions of what each means) and 32 examination items among the categories:

- leadership
- information and analysis
- strategic quality planning
- human resource utilization
- quality assurance of products and services
- quality results
- customer satisfaction.

Of all the categories, customer satisfaction attracts the highest number of points (300), followed by quality results and human resource utilization.

Federal Express Corporation was the first service company to win the award presented by the President of the USA. The company processes more than a million cargo items for shipment a day, which need tracking in a central information system. The company had a 'people–service–profit' philosophy which guided its policies and actions. It also had a well-formulated and deployed management evaluation system (survey–feed-back–action), involving questionnaires to employees, analysis of each work group's results by its manager and a discussion to formulate improvement plans and work on them. Aggregated data are produced for use in policy making.

Japan has its prestigious Deming Prize for Quality, named after the US statistician W.E. Deming and created in the 1950s. Winning such a prize requires a year-long preparation for a two-week review by examiners. Florida Power and Light was the first foreign company to win the award[7]. The process of applying for the prize caused it to take steps which enhanced progress. It had to show how the quality principles were being applied to improve performance. The self-audit description was a 900-page document. Only after that had been reviewed was the organization told that it could prepare for an on-site visit.

6.12 MEASURING CORPORATE AND INDIVIDUAL PERFORMANCE

There are rewards consequent upon an award which are valuable to the organization. It provides useful publicity material and offers a platform of quality on which to stand and proclaim the soundness of the organization and its products or services. As has been seen earlier, the various forms of award not only give a direction as to which areas an organization needs to improve in terms of quality; they also indicate possible ways in which those areas could be measured.

For example, Federal Express used to measure quality performance as the percentage of on-time deliveries, but now uses a 12-component measure. Each element is weighted to show how significantly it affects overall customer satisfaction. When a package changes hands, its bar code is scanned so that performance data can be tracked and analysed. Management meets daily to discuss the previous day's performance, and the quality components index has a cross-functional team dedicated to each element. It is headed by a senior executive so that improvements are made in each of the agreed areas. The 'service quality indicator' measurements are also linked into the corporate planning processes, forming the basis on which corporate executives are evaluated.

Individual performance objectives are set and monitored. Bonuses for executives are related to the performance of the whole organization in meeting the performance improvement goals. In addition, if employees do not give a rating to management leadership at least as high as the previous year, no executive will receive an end-of-year bonus.

There is clearly a need for this type of performance measurement, since relying on purely financial measures would not give an adequate indication of how the organization is performing. Royal Mail uses the EFQM model as an effective tool for measuring business success and monitoring improvement. Quality-oriented organizations are increasingly measuring part of their performance by their contribution to the community (as with the EFQM model). This does not mean just financially, but also socially and educationally.

A recent study[8] showed that directors' remuneration was related more to organizational size than to performance. If this is a true generalization, then directors have more of an incentive to pursue mergers and acquisitions rather than a course of action which has direct benefit to shareholders, workers or the economy as a whole. An important point to note is that corporate and individual performance need to be aligned in such a way that they do not contradict each other. Organizations which initially work so hard to show that continuous improvement to obtain quality does not necessarily mean job cuts can easily destroy goodwill by announcing them later. This has certainly happened with BT's 'Release' programme. A similar problem arose at British Airways when it asked for ideas to meet a cost reduction target of £150 million in 1993. This was in response to the company's top 150 executives being asked to reach a certain pre-tax profit figure which triggered their bonuses.

6.13 CONCLUSION

Leaders at all levels of an organization have to be certain to face outwards and communicate their quality strategy to all those other organizations that can affect it and are affected by it. Certainly, the way in which organizations treat their stakeholders becomes an advertisement for quality in itself. Benchmarking and various processes of accreditation are both ways of doing this. They also require the leader to face inwards to ensure that the lessons take hold. The next chapter addresses these needs.

ACTION QUESTIONS

- By what means (direct and indirect) does your organization demonstrate to its stakeholders that it has a quality strategy?
- How does the organization make sure that it is attuned to 'best practice' in its activities?
- Has your organization used any frameworks for accreditation? Are they integrated and have they had an impact on quality?

REFERENCES

1 Collins, T. (1993): 'BP in "more you save us more we pay you" deal', *Computer Weekly*, 25 March, p. 1.

2 Kanter, R.M. (1994): 'Collaborative Advantage: Successful Partnerships Manage the Relationship not just the Deal', *Harvard Business Review*, July/August, pp. 96–108.

3 Garvin, D.A. (1988): *Managing Quality*, The Free Press, New York, USA.

4 BT Forum (1993): *BT Today*, October, p. 9.

5 Camp, R. (1989): *Benchmarking: The Search for Industry Best Practices that Lead to Superior Performance*, Quality Press, Wisconsin, USA.

6 Shrimsley, R. (1993): 'Nearly one in three has never heard of the Citizen's Charter', *Daily Telegraph*, 26 August, p. 6.

7 Yoffee, L. (1990): 'Culture Change: the Common Goals', *Total Quality Management Magazine*, August, pp. 229–32.

8 Centre for Economic Performance (1993): *The Disappearing Relationship between Directors' Pay and Economic Performance*, London School of Economics, London, UK.

CHAPTER 7

The role of the leader: facing in

7.1 INTRODUCTION

Not only do leaders have to meet a set of expectations from the world outside to ensure that quality is perceived by those who affect the organization; they also need to look inside to see how these external demands will impact on their staff. The leader then has a boundary management job, constantly monitoring and changing the limits of what needs to be done. Looking in and looking out at the same time and managing the pressures and tensions this creates will call for much resilience. The key role is to make sure that quality does not fail the organization and that the organization does not fail the quest for quality. In Rank Xerox, it was said that no area of company activity remained unaffected by its customer satisfaction strategy.

7.2 COMMUNICATING STRATEGY AND VALUES INTERNALLY

Some strong views[1] on how leaders' actions are perceived are held by the CEO of Scandinavian Airline System (SAS):

> Leaders should be aware of how far non-verbal communication can go in illustrating the style that others in the organization should follow. And, in so doing, the leader will be helping to create the very image that the organization presents to its customers.

One anecdote quoted was an incident relating to boarding a plane at the end of the CEO's visit to an airport. Staff seemed uneasy until one member mentioned to him that they were waiting for him to board. The CEO replied that he had not heard an announcement. This was correct, since the staff were expecting him to choose his seat first before boarding the passengers. If the CEO indicated by his actions that he was superior to the customers, the organization could hardly call itself market-oriented!

At Royal Mail the role of communicating strategies and values internally is assisted by its leadership charter, which sets out the behaviours expected of Royal Mail's managers. Specifically, it says that a leader:

● provides a clear vision which aligns with the mission and values and captures the imagination
● describes the vision in simple language and frequently checks under-standing
● translates the vision into measurable goals which stretch the leader and teams and also challenge convention.

This is only a small part of the charter which every manager has and usually displays in the office with Royal Mail's values, and is the basis on which they operate.

7.3 ENABLING UNITS TO CREATE THEIR OWN MISSION

The mission and value statements referred to in Chapter 4 need to be retranslated into progressively smaller units of endeavour within the organization to make them meaningful. Rover has carried this process to the point where each group has assessed its contribution to the overall mission and goals and created its own mission (assuming the same underlying values) which is displayed in visible places. This allows a more focused approach and is more meaningful as staff can directly relate their activities to it. For example, when the Metropolitan Police produced a set of ten values as part of their change programme, the key question asked was: 'What noticeable difference will they make to the motivation and morale of the constable on the beat?' (or, indeed, to anyone employed in any sector). Some would argue for a reduced number of such values and goals, so that they can easily be remembered on a day-to-day basis, without written reminders.

7.4 FORWARD PLANNING OF QUALITY INITIATIVES

While major programmes may have been started by a central steering committee or group (Chapter 2), they nevertheless have to be rolled out by individuals leading the operating units. Furthermore, these units may themselves start their own initiatives which need to have an anchor point and be integrated within the overall planning of the company.

At Royal Mail, for example, the corporate business plan covers the activities of the whole organization. However, there are other planning activities, such as product development, carried out by the major business streams, but which depend on each of the geographic divisions and their functions for implementation. Each strategy steering group consists of functional directors and a planner, who are able to identify resource requirements as well as leaders of the various focus groups. For example, the quality strategy steering group draws on its quality focus groups to identify, review and recommend initiatives within the group's area of activity which are then passed up to the strategy steering group for appraisal. It can be seen that this requires the leader to operate upwards, laterally and downwards for any quality initiative so that he or she is at once driving and being driven by it. The planning process ensures that the checks and balances are inbuilt. This itself sets off the goal-setting process discussed below.

7.5 GOAL SETTING AND OBJECTIVES

The challenge for the organization is to identify a few major goals and use the quality process to cascade these down the organization. That way, senior managers will find it easier to check them and to ask the right questions. Leaders have to translate the overall goals into objectives for the individual work unit or team. These goals for quality may be derived from many different sources within the organization: quality councils, customer feedback surveys or retention rates, to name but a few. A useful guide[2] is to generate a matrix based on two key questions:

- Is the aim to improve service to the *external* or *internal* customer?
- Should *small* or *large* problems be tackled? (Small would normally be defined as failure to adhere to standards in everyday work, such as responding to the telephone within three rings; large would be the inadequate supply of a product or service, for example, installing a sophisticated new telephone system.)

This yields a quadrant of external (large and small problems) and internal (large and small problems) which helps to identify where the majority of the difficulties lie. Next, it is a question of choosing these in a systematic way and against certain key criteria: impact on the customer; support for the business plan; added value to the business; support for the mission statement and values and so on.

The important thing about these goals is that they have to be meaningful. People tend to be more committed to goals which they set for themselves. Otherwise they tend to avoid them or rebel against them. With flatter hierarchies, closer contact and teamworking, goals can be set more collaboratively. Those who are self-employed, for example, may feel a greater sense of satisfaction as they set up their plans, act on and measure and control them. This 'plan–do–control' cycle is at the heart of the quality management philosophy: I am checking on myself to improve what I do, rather than my manager doing it. If I find a problem, then I go to my manager or team for help. This form of goal setting requires the kind of managerial style described in Chapter 4, 4.9.

Some of the frameworks mentioned in Chapter 6 provide a natural priority list for goal setting, especially those where current performance needs lifting. However, these approaches have their critics, who would say that the awards give high marks to companies that demonstrate outstanding quality processes without always ensuring that the products and services are of a high calibre.

Results-driven programmes[3] have been shown to offer the best chance of success. In 1988 the chairman of General Electric (GE) used a results-driven approach across the whole organization called 'Workout'. The aim was to overcome factors which interfered with the organization's responsiveness, in particular bureaucracy and poor business procedures. The programme started with working sessions with a large cross-section of employees to identify a number of quick wins in target areas. These were things that employees could take on immediately to generate measurable improvement. For example, to get products to customers more quickly, employees worked jointly with customers and a trucking company to schedule, in advance, regular delivery dates for certain customers. Because of its success, the scheduling system was widely extended within the company. As each project achieves results, additional projects are launched, building on the confidence which develops from previous successes.

However, having results-driven improvement processes does not imply that senior management abdicates responsibility for difficult strategic decisions which may be necessary for the company's survival and prosperity. For example, GE's 'Workout' process complemented, but was no substitute for, the CEO's major restructuring and downsizing moves.

The importance of results should be highlighted directly. British Airways Group managing director, accompanied by the HR director and a member of the BA Trades Union Council, conduct walkabouts, and the objectives of the airline are communicated as:

- *quality* (improve on this, as it is what distinguishes us from the competition)
- *efficiency* (finding new ways of delivering value to customers cost-effectively)
- *profits*
- *success* (sharing the success of the company with employees and shareholders through dividends and investing for the future).

Similarly, the Rover Group developed its results orientation from a platform of quality management which focused on five critical success factors.

7.6 DECIDING WHAT TO MEASURE

Just as one has to be selective about the goals to work towards, there is also a need to really decide what aspects of meeting the goal are important. The goal of customer satisfaction, for example, can have many facets: it may be necessary to measure aspects such as dissatisfaction and retention rates as well as direct perceptions of satisfaction. A caution here is that if everything is measured people become wary of collecting information and become overwhelmed by it.

Quality management may also generate activities, measurements and reports which may not add value to the customer or to the company. At CIBA-Geigy, bureaucracy is defined as all those things that do not add such value. What is measured therefore must be directly relevant to strategic and other goals, not be what is merely nice to know.

Benchmarking will yield some ideas for what to measure. For example, in its initial recovery stage, Rank Xerox[4] discovered that it would need a year on year growth rate of 18 per cent to catch up with the Japanese in getting a new product to market. It also involved five times as many engineers, four times the number of design changes and three times the cost. This example provided a wealth of areas to examine and the indicators with which to do it.

Royal Mail chose six areas in which to monitor the quality process:

1 *Customer satisfaction index* (business and domestic customers are asked by a third party for their views on Royal Mail's performance against a number of specific elements determined by the customers themselves. These elements are reviewed every two years to see that they are up to date.

2 *Quality of service standards* (monthly monitoring of the percentage of mail delivered against published standards for Royal Mail).

3 *Comparative customer satisfaction survey* (quarterly survey against public utility and other benchmark companies such as Marks and Spencer, British Airways, W.H. Smith, and the Halifax Building Society).

4 *Employee opinion survey* (rolling programme every six months, covering half of the employees, to assess satisfaction and morale).

5 *Effective leadership feedback system* (assessing team leaders by upward as well as downward assessment, based especially on the leadership charter).

6 *Percentage involvement of employees in improvement projects* (there are hundreds of small groups).

The results in these areas are embedded in the internal management processes of the organization. For example, in divisional management meetings, planning and appraisal reference is made to these topics as they form the basis of divisional and other targets.

In decentralized organizations, measurement becomes more important as units conduct their own affairs. Employers at all levels need to understand the targets and how they are measured. In SAS, for example[5], there is a need to measure the results of staff (such as baggage handlers) who may not come into direct contact with customers, yet whose energy and commitment are vital behind the scenes.

7.7 SELECTING THE INDICATORS

Selecting the actual indicators can be a delicate task if they are not to mislead. The debate over the National Health Service shows the complexity of the matter, which is all the more obvious because it has a much publicized Patient's Charter. For example, the 1993 figures showed that the total number of people waiting for an operation on the NHS was higher than ever before, even if the duration individuals had to spend on waiting lists had been reduced. The British Medical Association said that there was evidence that hospital managers were influencing doctors in such a way that hospitals may not have been putting patients on the waiting lists at all. Indeed, some would say that the selection of the indicator of global waiting time was flawed. As one doctor put it: 'Waiting for a coronary bypass may be a shorter process, but it puts you at far more risk than waiting for a varicose vein operation.'

The measurement field is full of sayings such as 'People do what you review' and 'If you can't measure it you can't manage it'. However, warnings against this[6] are that we must be cautious about focusing only on the visible signs of performance in goal setting: what of the invisible parts relating to performance measurement? For example, there are the customers who do not complain, the patients who go elsewhere and the public who withdraw their support from the efforts of their local authority, educational institution and police service. The latter areas are particularly important, since without local cooperation their very existence is undermined. Their input for improvements and goodwill will be lost immediately and is unlikely to be regained in the long term.

Secondly, such preoccupation with figures can lead to a false sense of security of having goals which may detract from the overall quality of performance[7]. Maintaining a safe traffic flow is such an example. Counting the number of people who dare to drive down part of a bus lane due to poor positioning of bus stops and traffic lights in relation to a one-way system may be less useful than issuing warnings for dangerous parking, although the productivity measured in numbers may be easier to obtain in the former situation. Thirdly, if people are always given targets for everything they do they will see no reason to exceed them and do the minimum amount of work.

Finally, goal setting may rest on assumptions which are unquestioned by managers. For example, if average performance targets are met, by definition it means that half the employees will not meet the standard, generating dissatisfaction and high turnover. The key point here is that variation in performance is inevitable but it is how it is handled managerially which makes the difference to a quality-oriented company.

7.8 AGREEING INDICATORS WITH STAFF

At SAS the cargo division had measured the precision of its delivery as the cargo arriving at its destination with its paperwork attached to it. An error was recorded only if these became separated. A job was well done if the items stayed together, no matter how late the consignment arrived. All the while, the targets were met, but customers started complaining. So the cargo people were charged with devising a more relevant way of measuring their service quality performance in terms of its precision: speed of answering the telephone; meeting promised deadlines; cargo arriving on the booked plane; and the time of the plane landing to the time the cargo was ready for collection by the customer. Each terminal had to publish these measurements monthly, and this initially generated internal criticism (some staff were rewarded and others had to explain their shortcomings) even though the staff had designed this system themselves. However, it later came to be recognized as a valuable tool for highlighting problems which people did not always know existed and enabling them to find solutions.

There are some useful guidelines which, although applied to teams, could equally apply to individuals. They are:[8]

- The measurement system should be to help a team rather than top management gauge its progress.
- An empowered team must play the lead role in designing its own measurement system.
- If a team is responsible for a value delivery process which cuts across several functions it must create measures to track that process.
- A team should adopt only a handful of measures.

A useful distinction made here was in *results measures* (which tell an organization where it is in relation to its goals but not how it arrived there) and *process measures* (which monitor the tasks and activities that produce a given result). Results measures, while helping managers to keep a score on business performance, do not say what teams need to do to improve performance. Process measures, on the other hand, do. An example cited was that knowledge that the average time spent per service call rose by 15 per cent and as a result the number of late calls rose by 10 per cent would explain to technicians what the problem was, and why service costs had gone up and customer satisfaction and profits had been reduced.

Another point made by the study was that building a measurement system also helps in creating a team. This is because if members approach it with different perspectives and from different functions they create a common language. This in turn helps them to understand the team's goals in the same way and also set subgoals. Arguing through what the proposed measures track and why they are important helps to share knowledge and predicts problems which could arise in their interpretation.

7.9 AVOIDING OVER-MEASUREMENT

Measuring for measurement's sake is to be avoided at all costs. One cannot act on all measures at once and it lays the organization open to the charge that this is just another form of bureaucracy: 'We have to record but nothing gets done!' The ultimate test is to see how the measures feed back into the organization's main goals and the value they are adding to the customer. What management is seeking is an understanding of whether the business is continuously creating value. For those organizations which want to know this, there are the concepts of customer and employee loyalty, customer retention and the processes that go into achieving which can provide a useful guide to avoiding over-measurement. One employer in the credit card industry has a scorecard of more than 20 different measurements which the organization believes to be factors in customer retention. On the days when the 95 per cent targets are achieved, money goes into the bonus pool and news is posted throughout the organization. This ensures that it has one of the highest levels of staff loyalty and profitability in the business.

Perhaps the acid test of the measures is when they cease to be important to either customers or staff – that is, they fail to motivate to achieve or improve on the previous attainment. This may be because the staff have come to the conclusion that the measures are irrelevant to measuring the adequacy of their performance to the ultimate consumer.

7.10 CREATING THE INTERNAL NETWORK

Inevitably there will be pockets of resistance within the organization which will view quality with suspicion or, if not, have a neutral attitude towards it. A good leader at any level of the organization will know that it is important to create a critical mass of supporters as 'opinion leaders' before the change. These individuals will form an 'emotional support group' and be better able to discard the anxieties that often accompany new ways of working.

The network is also useful in sharing feedback of what is working well, where and why. Alternatively, if things are not going according to plan, there is an early warning system of problems and also a band of committed people who will do their utmost to overcome them.

The network is also a very effective way of checking out the next steps in rolling programmes. An internal organization network can span countries, locations, functions and levels, enabling test sites to be chosen where there is the greatest chance of success. This can then act as an anchor point for the subsequent roll-out.

7.11 DEVELOPING THE INTERNAL CUSTOMER PHILOSOPHY

All quality management programmes stress the importance for their success of considering those with whom we deal in organizations as internal customers, with their own needs, expectations and requirements for excellence. All parts of the organization give and receive a service. If the organization cannot deliver quality internally to its own staff, it will certainly be unable to do so to the external customer. Staff preoccupied with their own problems cannot focus outwards.

This philosophy is at its most crucial in industries or sectors where the majority of staff may have little or no direct contact (face to face or by telephone) with the external customer and not see how they are adding value. For example, the insurance industry will normally have a large 'back office' where all the processing of documents and policies is done. One relatively small error or numerical miscalculation can generate extra problems which push up the cost of the transaction or, worse still, result in a complaint or loss of customer. In fact, as from January 1995 all companies selling life insurance have to indicate how many hundreds of pounds per thousand of business transacted goes on costs. This will then signal to purchasers which organizations are being inefficient yet charging higher premiums. Ultimately this will be used as another competitive weapon.

Some organizations have realized the importance of identifying an end customer for their staff. Take the job of a garage mechanic servicing a car. Typically, reception handles the papers and the mechanic does the work and never meets the customer. In some places, however, the mechanics drive the car round to the customer (a welcome short break) and can explain briefly what was done. They come to know the regular customers and the latter, when asked to fill in the evaluation form, may feel more involved, since their ratings may well affect someone's livelihood.

The consideration given to finding out the needs of the external customer should also be applied to the internal customer. Each interface in the chain has to be carefully managed if the service is to be successfully delivered to the customer. Each unit within the organization can ask itself (as some organizations do): Who are my customers? What do they want from me? Do I give them what they need? Can I do better? Royal Mail emphasizes the idea that, as the staff are internal customers, the managers should support them and also be judged by what they (as customers) think of them. The interesting point here is that this is supported by a 360-degree appraisal (see Chapter 5), an appropriate structure which de-emphasizes boundaries (Chapter 3) and a culture which permits a supportive management style (Chapter 4).

Internally there are often departments with a support role which may be seen as somehow 'outside' the process, such as human resources, finance and accountancy or catering. However, they still need to be brought into the system. One wrong grading or inaccurate pay or tax assessment raises an outcry, as the fact is that these things are expected to be right first time, every time and are usually taken for granted.

7.12 TEAMWORKING FOR CONTINUOUS IMPROVEMENT

Increasingly now in quality-oriented companies, there is an emphasis on working in teams. There are many forms that teams can take: some are permanent; others temporary, with a special purpose or limited life; some come together to span an interface between separate functions so that the process of adding value appears seamless to the customer. The rationale given is broad:

- They provide faster response and flexibility in the face of market changes compared to totally functional units.
- They encourage multi-competence and enhanced, all-round skills.
- They demand networking, cooperation and integration of functions thus avoiding destructive parochialism.

● They bring greater resources to problem solving.

The process of information sharing, joint problem solving, giving and receiving support, commitment to a cause (here customer satisfaction) all help to weld a team and enhance performance.

The sort of behaviours that are visible when a team is operating effectively (as opposed to merely being a group) are:

● *commitment* (to the purpose and value of the outcome);
● *loyalty* (to each other as people and in helping each other in times of difficulty);
● *inclusion* (being part of something important and bigger than oneself);
● *pride* (in the purpose and membership of the group);
● *trust* (in each other's abilities and integrity).

These may appear 'soft' characteristics to measure, but their absence is easily detectable: communications break down; the group forms sub-groups; internal rivalry occurs; and the main task becomes secondary to individuals' own goals.

Emphasis on teamworking may in some cases be seen as a threat to existing methods of representation for a number of reasons[9]. First, it encourages staff to drop their identity with a trade or profession and focus on the production or delivery of a particular product or service. Secondly, staff are more likely to approach their supervisor or team leader with a problem rather than the union representative. Management also bypasses the union organization by using direct communication to staff. Fourthly, teamwork tends to remove work organization matters from the area of collective bargaining. For example, payment by piecework or results may soon be seen as not fitting in with the new ways of working. Finally, since employers are encouraging people to develop a portfolio of skills congruent with the production needs of the business, it is more difficult for unions to define their membership around particular occupations or grades (whose numbers are themselves reduced).

Lucas Aerospace[10] is one organization which had to change from an old shopfloor culture with payment by results for components, regardless of quality (inspected in at the end). The new culture required concern for the customer and reorganization into product-based teams working on families of similar components. Flexibility between work tasks was needed as well as participation in continuous improvement. These changes were won by conceding certain union requests such as harmonization of employment conditions between white- and blue-collar workers, a shorter working week and no redundancies. The shop stewards still have a role to play (although they were initially concerned at seeing their constituencies broken up as employees joined different teams), but they then established new ones. The role has evolved from tending to oppose any changes to being more proactive, and as a committee they are in communication with management far more than was the case in the past.

On the service side, BT's Personal Communications Business Group recently launched a programme to help customer-facing teams to improve service[11]. Using existing surveys and customer satisfaction measures, they are regularly interviewed by independent market research companies. The results of Focused Customer Feedback is given monthly to management meetings and discussed with the teams. At these meetings, staff have a chance to review their performance. The feedback allows target-setting for first line managers and a better understanding of customer requirements.

7.13 EMPOWERMENT

New forms of working for quality require decisions to be made as low as possible down the organization to enable it to act speedily and flexibly. This is where the notion of empowerment has played a part. This is the situation where power and control is given to employees (as individuals or groups) who need it most for a particular task. It is unhelpful to talk of changes to be made but not giving enough power to carry them out. Managers who empower people are not abdicating their role as leaders as they are still there to provide resources and support (see Chapter 9). Empowerment is also something more than delegation of responsibility and authority. In the latter case, the manager decides what to delegate and the employee does it. With empowerment, the manager does not assume the role of expert and decide what should be done – rather, the employee can exert influence upwards to convince and reassure, and can use discretion, manage the risk within the guidelines and organizational values and innovate where necessary. Employees in this situation may well have access to information (previously known only to managers), on a need-to-know basis, for example customer profitability.

However, although organizations may wish to adopt an empowerment culture, there may be certain barriers to overcome. Employees may say that they do not want extra responsibility. They are not paid for it and that is the manager's job. Managers may feel that if they are not seen to be doing certain work they are not seen to be adding value. Or, they may believe that the decision or job could have been done in half the time. Then there is the risk factor that the failure may rebound or that the job may be done so well that the manager is shown up. All these difficulties are reduced if empowerment is seen as part of the learning organization looking for improvements (see Chapter 6). Empowerment allows staff to find out about the best ways of doing things, not just doing what they are told to do.

Much of the casework on empowerment has come from the USA, but UK-based organizations are also adopting this approach. Nissan UK and W.H. Smith are two of the pioneers here. Rank Xerox's motives were spurred by the need to devolve responsibility and accountability to those closest to the customers so that they could fix problems speedily without the need to seek authority. The spin-off effects were that it reduced the layers of management and also the cycle times for the process. Rover Group has also taken this route to the point where shift workers have put together a programme for maintenance (since they, not the trainers, are the experts), and more than 700 people have been trained in it although they still remain shift workers and receive no extra pay.

The CEO of Levi Strauss has commented that the manager in an empowering company has a much tougher role than before[12]. This is because a manager can no longer rely on title to get things done. Managers have to be clear and thoughtful about the standards that are going to be set (since these are the ones upon which the empowered employees will be basing their decisions). Perhaps the most telling aspect is summed up in the following quotation:

> You have to accept the fact that the decisions or recommendations may be different from what you would do. They could very well be better but they are going to be different. You have to be willing to take your ego out of it.

His view of employees was that most people want to make a contribution, but that organizations encourage bad habits such as politicking and parochialism which work against all of this.

7.14 MAINTAINING COMMITMENT

Maintaining commitment to a quality programme is far more difficult than getting started. Reasons for the failures of programmes were given in Chapter 2, and it is typically about one year to 18 months before doubts seem to surface, which is why programmes are constantly being refocused and renamed (Chapter 1). Certainly the quality culture (Chapter 4) will help to reinforce this, as well as the policies and processes outlined in Chapter 5, in particular, the careful use of and action upon the findings of staff surveys, training and self-managed learning. Three key themes for maintaining staff commitment are:

● consistency
● participation
● renewal
● reinforcement of results.

The first key factor which emerges is that of consistency, and employees are quick to spot discrepancies in any initiatives. For example, the mission and values statements and the way in which managers behave will be closely scrutinized. They will soon identify who receives reward and recognition: the people who play by the rules, or those who try to live up to the values and perhaps make a mistake. Communications is another area which can easily be misinterpreted or seen to be at odds with a policy or practice covered in the organization. A special aspect is the consistency of standards. Are they applied fairly and dispassionately across the unit or organization, or does expediency start to operate in times of difficulty? Another source of inconsistency is the attitude to problem solving. If a person raises a problem is it acknowledged, does the organization say 'It is our problem and we need to allocate resources to solve it', or does it assume that it is your problem and that you should do something about it?

Participation can take many forms. A recent survey[13] categorized them as:

● *direct communications* (written, verbal, briefing sessions, company newspapers);
● *problem solving* (tapping into employee knowledge and experience, quality groups and suggestion schemes);
● *financial participation* (profit sharing, value added team bonuses);
● *representative participation* (staff may be represented through unions or joint consultative committees).

The survey also identified a number of problems with managing employee participation. First was a lack of continuity due to the frequent career changes of managers who drove the schemes. Successors may have different priorities and not assume ownership. Secondly, there was often lack of support from middle management who are traditionally caught having to operate in two directions. Inappropriate schemes was another area criticized. This tended to happen when organizations bought into a package which was not 'fit for the purpose' and had not been linked into other organizational goals. Indeed, some often had conflicting objectives and methodologies or fell within several different functional areas (for example, personnel and marketing) and were not seen to be integrated into the business. Finally, there was the usual dose of workforce scepticism. The survey concluded that:

> although specific employee involvement schemes may be faddish, employee involvement itself seems a more permanent phenomenon, even if it takes a variety of forms.

Corning Glass's overall strategy for quality improvement explicitly uses participation as a building block[14]. For them, participation means active membership of a quality team. The CEO has said that he wants to raise the percentage of people involved from 61 per cent to 100 per cent. At present, people who are not in a team feel left out. What they have therefore communicated to employees is: 'We want to know what you think, your ideas, and we'll listen carefully to what you say'. If people understand that the organization really means it, they will flock to participate.

A third main theme in maintaining commitment is that of renewal. As was pointed out earlier, efforts towards quality are constantly being renewed. British Telecom has a programme[15] called 'Break Out' which is scheduled to last a couple of years and aimed at breaking the bonds of old ways of working. It builds on the gains made through the quality-related processes of putting the customer first and the leadership programme, and will remove barriers which constrain thinking. Some 20 priority areas have been singled out, to be tackled via five work streams (each having a more detailed definition):

- business objectives
- revenue generation

- business re-engineering
- organizational alignment (i.e. with the customer)
- people.

Without going into detail, each work stream has its own champion who is a member of the Quality Council. Teams are led by nominated full-time and part-time BT people, led by a stream director and supported by a consultancy. The 'Break Out' process also looked at some current initiatives and change programmes (more than 900) which may need to be reshaped or stopped altogether.

In conclusion, the momentum for sustaining commitment can come from outside or inside the organization. In the first instance, feedback comes from customers and suppliers, regulatory bodies and the benchmarking process. Internally, the missing values need to be restated and successful results widely communicated. The leader can facilitate all this by ensuring that the information from all these sources is received and coordinated.

7.15 ENSURING CONTINUOUS LEARNING

One of the roles of the leader is to look inwards to ensure that continuous improvement takes place. The various organization policies for this were covered in Chapter 5 under self-managed learning. However, managers at all levels can affect the success or otherwise of these initiatives, which depend on managerial support in a number of ways. The obvious one is the allocation of resources, and the provision of time to devote to this is important. For example, in some (not all) organizations, employees are encouraged to learn (as opposed to attend specific training courses) in company time through vehicles such as self-managed learning groups. Managers may have to make regular concessions to enable their staff to do this even when there may be an emergency job to be done. They may also have to accept that travel arrangements may need to be curtailed. Other resources to support this may be in terms of accommodation and access to company information and services.

Perhaps even more important than providing resources is the fact that managers will need to be supportive in handling the outputs from these initiatives. There may well be requests to alter roles, expand job opportunities or be given backing for a new idea, secondment or project which could add to the line manager's workload. However, if this kind of support is given reluctantly, or not forthcoming at all, the initiatives will die through lack of take-up.

7.16 REWARDING THE BEARERS OF BAD NEWS

In Chapter 4, 4.9, the importance of a leader's style in encouraging a problem-solving approach to continuous improvement was highlighted. The leader should be saying: 'Where are the difficulties? Let's root them out', rather than taking an attitude which is still very prevalent: 'Don't bring me problems, bring me solutions'. In fact, people tend to be rewarded for 'having things under control', 'running a tight ship', and always appearing successful so that problems are never visible. If staff are to really take their managers' word seriously and produce a list of problems, it must not be seen as an indication of their incompetence but rather as their vigilance. The willingness to do this depends on the organization saying: 'Although you appear to have the problem the owner is the organization, and therefore the solution is down to all of us to contribute in whatever way is appropriate'.

It is all too easy for those who criticize the organization from inside to be classified as troublemakers, disturbing the cosy illusions of top management who perhaps, in their prime introduced various products or services whose time has now passed. Falling sales or other indicators do nothing to convince these people, who find excuse after excuse to support their existence. Every organization needs its 'loyal rebels' who can take on this role – perhaps they are the most valuable employees of all. Otherwise, top management becomes surrounded with 'yes' people who will never be drawn for an opinion on anything. At GE Medical Systems, their 'Workout' procedure was designed to bring to the surface objections to and criticisms of existing processes across all functions, and to overcome a culture where blame and lack of trust flourished. The senior management then participated in a round table, listening to discussions which focused on ways to reorganize work and use more effectively the time of the individual, team and organization. The sessions ended with individuals and functional teams signing nearly 100 written contracts to implement the new procedures.

7.17 ENCOURAGING PROBLEM SOLVING

The leader's job of encouraging problem solving is made easier if there are organizational processes in place which encourage this. For example, AMEX carries out country and regional evaluations on key measures on card products: timeliness of processing basic applications, emergency card replacements and making up customer statements. This is designed to probe continuously for indications of customer dissatisfaction. Similarly, Westinghouse conducts a total quality fitness review at operating unit level. Each unit is rated against 12 criteria (conditions of excellence) which build from the base to an organization which meets total quality requirements. The rating on information will show whether the unit's required information is clear, complete, timely and so on. The reviews are voluntary and naturally the results are confidential. All levels in the organization are included. The reviewing team scores the items separately and reaches consensus on the final score. The quality centre which conducts the reviews offers follow-up services for the implementation of any actions arising.

While it is easier for the leader to encourage problem solving with the internal culture above, it is also easier if there is pressure from the external environment (see Chapter 3, customer feedback). The important thing when things go wrong is how good the organization is at recovery[16]. Three specific prescriptions are:

- Encourage customers to complain and make it easy for them to do so.
- Make timely personal communications with customers as a key part of the strategy.
- Encourage employees to respond effectively to customer problems and give them the means to do so.

When American Express cardholders telephone the number on their monthly statements, they talk to a highly experienced customer service representative with the authority to solve on the spot 85 per cent of the problems that prompt the telephone calls.

7.18 PROTECTING INNOVATION

Innovation is in one sense a special case of problem solving. Being asked to tackle something new is, in effect, being invited to make mistakes and put them right. A leader in a quality environment cannot always rely on continuous improvement being obtained incrementally, building on what has gone before (see Chapter 9 for a discussion of this issue). Sometimes a completely new idea, approach or process is required.

However, there are many direct and subtle organizational ways to kill an idea and dampen enthusiasm:

- let it die (do not even acknowledge its presence)
- say that it's been tried before or it's never been tried before
- shout that it's too expensive
- produce too many reasons why it can't work and find complications
- maintain that it doesn't fit in with the product range, company policy and so on.

It is all too easy for people and circumstances to combine to sink any creative ideas. The leader's job is to sense the organizational politicking and give the idea some room to flourish.

Then there are many blocks within individuals which may unintentionally stop innovation. Some people have never acquired a skill to isolate a problem in the first place. The core cannot be extracted from the context to identify the significant areas for improvement. Others may also use stereotyping to categorize problems or solutions and cannot break out of this set way of thinking. Employees may also be worried about having to confront different perceptions of their situation. As one senior manager once said to the author: 'Once we've opened up all the different views, how are we ever going to get agreement?' There may also be emotional reasons why people cannot release their creative side: fear of risk taking, inability to let fantasy rule; dislike of operating in a chaotic environment. The leader can help here by ensuring that people have the opportunity to access their creative side.

Equally, there may be a cultural environment that is unsupportive. Some organizations like decisions to follow a very rational, systematic process and become uncomfortable with intuitions or creative synthesis which have to await verification or which need an additional piece of information to complete the jigsaw. Or perhaps there may be a long while before feedback can be obtained and corrective action taken, as with long-term investment decisions. There may also be organizational taboos about a particular product or offering in which an individual or a powerful group have invested time and effort. Therefore to suggest an alternative possibility may threaten their very existence. The leader's role here is to help create a supportive environment by allowing constructive criticism and developing the necessary creative skills through access to tools and techniques. In particular, encouraging a questioning attitude, allowing expression to controversial or unusual ideas and at least giving them a hearing are the kind of behaviours required.

7.19 CONCLUSION

This chapter has been concerned with analysing the leader's role in quality, particularly when looking at what can be done inside the organization. To be successful, the leader needs to link together all the elements (mission statement, goals, standards, teamwork, problem solving and innovation) in ways which support, not contradict, each other. If the attitudes and behaviour of the leader are not consistent with the overall quality message being communicated, cynicism will set in. That is why it is important to subject the organization to self-assessment and benchmarking to ensure that the links are there and are achieving the desired result. Without them, the leader will find it difficult to make changes, which is the theme of the next chapter.

ACTION QUESTIONS

- How well do the leaders help to integrate corporate mission and values with local custom and practice? How do they achieve this?
- How do leaders decide what an effective measure of quality performance is? Are they derived through consultation or are they handed down?
- What skills and experience do leaders in your organization need to possess to encourage innovation?

REFERENCES

1 Carlzon, J. (1987): *Moments of Truth*, Ballinger Publishing Company, Wisconsin, USA.

2 Ezerman, G.C. (1991): 'The Quality Quadrant: Which Quality Problems do we Tackle First?' In Mastenbroek, W.F, *Managing for Quality in the Service Sector*, Blackwell, Oxford.

3 Schaffer, R.H. and Thompson, H.A. (1992): 'Successful Change Programmes Begin with Results', *Harvard Business Review*, January/

February, pp. 80–9.

4 Walker, R. (1992): 'Rank Xerox: Management Revolution', *Long Range Planning*, **25**(1), pp. 9–21.

5 Carlzon, J. (1993), op. cit.

6 Deming, W.E. (1982): *Quality Productivity and Competitive Position*, MIT Centre for Advanced Engineering, Cambridge, Massachusetts, USA.

7 Clark, F.A. (1992): 'Public Awareness', *Total Quality Management Magazine*, December, pp. 373–8.

8 Meyer, C. (1994): 'How the Right Measures Help Teams Excel', *Harvard Business Review*, May/June, pp. 95–103.

9 Geary, J.F. (1993): 'Workgroups and Participation', *European Participation Monitor*, No.5, pp. 8–11.

10 Hartwright, C. and Taylor, C (1993): 'Total Teamwork at Lucas Aerospace', *European Participation Monitor*, No.5, pp. 11–22.

11 British Telecom, 'So How Good is Your Team?', *BT Today*, p. 20.

12 Howard, R. (1990): 'Values Make the Company: An interview with Robert Haas', *Harvard Business Review*, September/October, pp. 133–44.

13 Marchington, M., Wilkinson, A. and Ackers, P. (1993): 'Waving or Drowning in Participation?', *Personnel Management*, March, pp. 46–9.

14 Houghton, J.R. (1991): 'World Class Quality', *Total Quality Management Magazine*, February, pp. 27–31.

15 British Telecom (1993): 'Big Push for the Ideal Customer Experience', *BT Today*, December, pp. 4–5.

16 Berry, L., Ziethaml, V.A. and Parasuraman, A. (1990): 'Five Imperatives for Improving Service Quality', *Sloan Management Review*, **31**(iv), Summer, pp. 29–38.

Leading the change

8.1 INTRODUCTION

The way in which the book has been structured so far suggests that when the strategy, structure, culture and policies are all in place and the leaders have assessed their inward- and outward-facing roles, then change can begin. The reality is very different, as every change practitioner knows. Once the change has been set in motion, many things (however much planning has been done) are found wanting or not quite consistent and new ways have to be found of implementing policies or changing working conditions. At every level, the leader's role is to recognize when things need modifying and who can offer support, while moving forward in the agreed general direction.

8.2 SKILLS OF THE CHANGE AGENT

Those in a leadership role within their organization not only have their functional job to carry out but also have to adopt the mantle of a change agent, recognizing that how things were done before may be at considerable odds with what is now required and that they will have to manage the transition. The role may be uncomfortable in that the leader is taking people into uncharted waters, needing their collective resolve to steer in the right direction and overcome any difficulties. It may also be uncomfortable in that leaders are unsure whether they have the right skills, have enough of each of them and are confident of applying them in a timely way. In this situation the leader may have to relinquish any sense of being an expert, thinking of the role as one of a catalyst but one which will not be unchanged by the experience.

So what are the skills of the change agent? They are many and varied, and are essentially those of an internal consultant. Therefore sensitivity to the existing culture must be the bedrock on which to operate. The culture needs to be harnessed or altered to drive through the change across the business. This calls for characteristics such as persistence and emotional resilience in the face of difficulties or disappointments. The skills are often grouped in the following way:

- *entry* (obtaining access and a hearing from those who need to be influenced);
- *relationship building* (establishment of trust and rapport);
- *diagnostic* (understanding of the situation through careful questioning and unbiased listening);
- *influencing* (looking for agreement to proposals for action and gaining commitment);
- *transition* (helping the process of change to take place; facilitation).

However, underlying these generic skills are others. The change agent has to be analytical to define the problems and needs of the situation and of the clients (staff, peers and managers). Communication skills for ensuring clarity in these situations and uncovering people's needs, exploring issues and signalling the way forward are vital. The change agent also has to draw upon the innovation and problem-solving skills covered in the previous chapter so that people will have confidence in overcoming difficulties and ensuring that continuous learning takes place.

8.3 IDENTIFYING KEY PEOPLE

A first step is to identify the key people in the process. Stakeholder analysis is a useful technique for first listing all those who have an interest in the outcome of the change and then assessing on a two-by-two grid how important they are and how certain the change agents are that they understand them. For example, if the stakeholders are important but the change agents are uncertain of the views they hold, they may need to ask other stakeholders to help clarify the situation; feed back the information and perhaps influence them directly.

Some people may not be so obviously identified, and that is where group brainstorming will come in useful. There may be individuals or groups at operational stages in the overall process who can exert a disproportionate or a critical influence over the outcomes and who, by their involvement, can help or hinder the process. Customers or suppliers may be willing to be more tolerant when major changes are taking place if it is explained to them that in the long term these changes are for their benefit.

8.4 ENTRY

In the 'entry' part of the process, several issues need to be addressed: anxiety, trust and credibility. Anxiety is likely to exist simply because there is a new path to be trodden. Airing concerns in a structured way is a good place to start. Managers can do this with their teams just as consultants can do it with the client.

Trust is vital and the change agent's (consultant or facilitator) motives and willingness to genuinely assist the processes will be evident, even if there is some scepticism as to the possible outcome. This will also depend on the credibility of the change agent themselves and their perceived sponsor. People carry stereotypes of others at a given moment in time, either ignoring or being unaware of previous competence or experience. Often the same message delivered by line managers will seem more credible simply because they are 'one of us' and they know our situation. Credibility is also something ongoing, put to the test in how well difficulties are overcome. These three areas are not static; they need to be continuously reviewed.

8.5 ESTABLISHING THE CONTRACT

Once the stakeholders have been correctly identified and their needs and concerns assessed, it is crucial to establish a 'psychological contract' with them so that they are prepared to work with the changes rather than against them. A crucial area is convincing employees that continually improving and new ways of organizing work will not result in job losses.

In Royal Mail's various changes related to quality improvement and reorganization, the guarantees employees wanted were no compulsory redundancies. Management could not give this, although they made it clear that these would be avoided where at all possible. As it happened, there were none. Reductions were achieved through the normal turnover of staff and voluntary retirement.

Contracting involves the sharing of control and determining or reclassifying objectives and measures (see Chapter 1, 1.3 and Chapter 7, 7.5), agreeing a method of working and what activities need to be carried out and just what role both parties play in the process. The team leader can do this, as can managers at a more senior level in the organization where the problems may be broader and more complex.

8.6 RECOGNIZING INHIBITORS OF CHANGE

To some extent, the inhibitors of change are the opposite of those factors needed to protect innovation (see Chapter 7, 7.18). They may be classified as cultural, organizational and personal. Here the leader's role is to anticipate these reactions before they become too entrenched.

The cultural inhibitors of change are the cynicism, apathy, and destructive behaviour which may set in at the first signs of difficulty or the unanticipated. There may be cultural beliefs and norms here, such as 'Change happens all the time', so that fatigue sets in immediately a new initiative is announced. Conversely, change may be unusual, so that people pretend things are not going to happen. Then, there are the cultural war stories, such as 'We've tried all this before and it failed', so the change agent has to start from a negative set of expectations, neutralize them so that people are at least prepared to try and then turn them into a positive experience. This is a classic situation for consultants, who must identify how the restraining forces[1] retard the impetus to change.

The organizational inhibitors of change may be the horizontal strata within an organization. Typically, this is middle management who have to make the broad guidelines issued from above work at the more detailed level for those whom they manage. Obviously this will depend on the styles of management they are able to deploy, and the recognition of the difficulty of this task is enough to make them resistant to moving ahead. The other main concern of this group is justifying their added value. They are not adding value through strategic direction, nor are they usually customer-facing and therefore seen as contributing directly to the organization's core activities. They are fearful of being seen without a role.

Functional or structural groups may also be inhibitors of change. The habits formed in the job (the ease or speed of doing things, the fact that this led to a feeling of safety and comfort in not making mistakes and therefore not being punished but nearly always rewarded) locks people into old patterns of working. Secondly, fear of the unknown, real or imagined, will paralyse them, as will the felt absence of skills to cope or simply organizational inertia. The old ways of approving a project or resolving conflict are easier to handle than the new ways with their teething problems. Finally, resistance from this group may be due to the sunk costs already invested in the old organization structure or ways of working.

At an individual level, people may have predisposed feelings towards change, such as 'It never really changes anything' or 'Change just means more work'. There may well be feelings of insecurity, such as 'What will happen to my job, status, power, boss, reward?', and so on. At this level, there are feelings of distrust, as everyone is looking over his or her shoulder and asking the question 'What is in it for me?' Credible sources of information are sought and are a distraction to the main work as rumours and counter-rumours abound. This is where the leader should be filling in the vacuum.

8.7 KNOWING IF HELP IS NEEDED

There are times when change programmes need assistance from outside for a variety of reasons, and consultants or facilitators are called in. Often, when senior managers discover problems in the organization they look for direct or simple solutions, see 'more training' or 'better communications' as the solution and contact the training department. When this does not work they call in the consultant, who needs to check out the definition of the problem in the first place and adopt a suitable role.

There are several different roles which the consultant may play in helping to assess the client. He or she may decide to be the:

- *expert* (providing specific input which the client's organization does not have);
- *sounding board* (generally a confidante with whom the client can talk through the situation and try out options, using the consultant's experience from outside);
- *project leader* (leading some part of the change because of special expertise which is later to be handed on);
- *group facilitator* (the consultant may join to help them work better on the task in hand);

- *collaborator* (the consultant may join in a group to provide the missing skill or experience in the overall group mix).

The important thing is that both parties should be clear about which role is being played and what the limitations are for each of them. The classic case is when the client expects to receive 'recommendations' from an expert who plays the role of a facilitator or a sounding board. This leads to frustration and disappointment in the gap between the ideal solution required and the practical realities of what can be implemented.

8.8 MANAGING EXTERNAL CONSULTANTS

One of the key factors in managing external consultants is establishing the role and relationships at the outset, as in the previous section. This will also affect the form the output is going to take (report, discussion document, series of action learning milestones and so forth). The consultant needs to be very clear in the assignment (for the purposes of reporting) who is the actual client and who is the individual sponsor or group. Consultants traditionally always seek the top decision maker, but the reality is that the day-to-day contact (depending on the intervention) may have to be lower down the organization. If this is the case, the consultant needs to be mindful not only of how the relationship with the client is handled but also how the client handles the relationship with the sponsors and whether the client welcomes assistance in this.

The CEO of Scandinavian Airline System has summed up the dilemma of when to hire consultants. Sometimes, he says, it is 'a point of honour' to be able to handle a situation without using outside consultants. This notion arises from a view that the manager has superior knowledge, does not make mistakes and needs to be in total control all the time. His view is that if he gives responsibility to his staff he must allow them to bring in the extra resources needed, and all that matters is that the ideas have worked. However, there may be many reasons for hiring a consultant, an experienced person will want to explore not only the 'logical' reasons but also the possible political ones which will affect how any findings from the assignment are interpreted and investigated.

It is important that both the client and the consultant are partners in the diagnostic stage and that they accept the distinction between the felt need and what may have later appeared to be the real problem. For example, the poor communications which may have been the original basis for calling in a consultant in the first place may really have its origins in a culture of competitiveness reinforced by a rigid structure where budgets are met to the detriment of overall performance and an unwillingness to share information exists. Thus it is vital that the boundaries of the problem be defined and that it is agreed what areas are open for investigation and what information will be forthcoming.

By working together, the consultant is including the client in the learning process and vice versa. It then becomes more obvious why one course of action is more appropriate than another because the rationale has been made apparent to both parties. Even if the diagnosis has some negative elements, a potentially hostile reaction is likely to be reduced because of the shared understanding. This, in turn, means that the manager as an internal champion will be more confident of the position and better able to convince other parts of the organization of the validity of the findings.

In terms of implementation, the consultant may or may not be invited to have an input. In any case, it is likely that the involvement of the consultant will be less, as the client by now will be taking full ownership of the situation. In fact, a good consultant should be planning an exit. Selling on extra time might be of short-term benefit, but the client, in a long-term or even discontinuous relationship with the consultant, will recognize integrity and this will be a plus factor when additional work comes up for tender.

It should be axiomatic that, in an organization committed to continuous improvement, the processes surrounding the use of external consultants needs to be reviewed. It is all too easy to blame an external consultant for failures or to prove that internal problems will not succumb even to an outside expert. Some organizations' view of external consultants is 'Make sure they leave something behind', otherwise there is no transference of skills or organizational growth. The less ethical consultant will just be encouraging a climate of more dependence, until suddenly the intervention has become obsolete and this signals the death of the relationship anyway. It is a no-win situation. As the organization learns it asks more questions of itself, and in the long term that is what generates more work for the consultant.

It goes without saying that an organization should make careful preparation for using consultants. Some recommendations for using them will say 'Clearly define your objective before having them in the first place'. It is not always so clear-cut, and if the organization can do this so precisely, perhaps it does not need consultants in the first place. The point is well taken though, and in complex situations, a consultant may spend a short time getting to grips with the problem with the client and perhaps redefine or set new boundaries for the assignment so that precise objectives can be drawn up and also agreed with the various parties internally. Proper briefing is essential – that is, time and resources should be allocated so that the consultant understands the problem both at the tendering stage and at the start of the project, as situations can change very rapidly.

Naturally, CVs, previous experience and referees need to be questioned and fees and expenses or other conditions agreed explicitly to avoid disagreement later. Bidders should also be given sufficient time to prepare a bid. Although responsiveness is important, if key people are out of the country a thoughtful proposal will not be submitted: it will either be delegated or be 'off the shelf'. Presentations by consultants should leave enough time for questions, and it is helpful if the client plans approximately equal time for both parties. Three tenders is probably the maximum number to seek, as then people feel they are in with a chance.

8.9 WORKING IN THE POWER STRUCTURE

Leading a change in quality cannot be done in a vacuum. There is always the question of whether the power and influence in the organization are supporting the initiative. In the quality management literature, little has been said about the political processes which help or hinder implementation; the emphasis has been on logical, empirically-based systems being implemented. Managers recognize, however, that any change is a highly political process. The sort of political resistance to be overcome may be found in an individual's or group's need for power and influence.

At the individual level are the personal needs for power and status related to self-image, superiority and need for control. Some of the individuals who are likely to be motivated in this way are easy to spot (the personalized number plates, the expensively furnished offices or the designer labels). Since these people actively display their status and power symbols for people to immediately recognize, they may affect an air of approachability and affability to offset the nature of their true inner needs.

After all, if everyone can see the outward signs of power they have made their point and can afford to be nice (until someone actually says 'no'). Then there is another group, motivated by power but unable to display it openly for fear of challenge or confrontation. These are more difficult to spot since they manage to distance themselves from any firm decision by means such as selecting a more junior person for a post which they feel able to manipulate or avoiding having any firm opinion (under the guise of reasonable impartiality!) so that they are never actually caught on the wrong side.

Since both these 'types' have usually been found out or have made enemies, they can be identified when plans for change are being drawn up. The skilful change agent can either go around them or give them a role in the change which will suit their needs, personality and skill levels (which, incidentally, may be low – the more intellectually challenged they are, the more political they need to be to compensate and survive in their positions).

Another problem with political people is that they may be overdependent on others. Change may be a threat. They may lose their sponsor or power base (for example, information or other resource) and may be fearful of being cut adrift. Or the change could actually disturb a bid for more power or open up their power to others.

At a group level, change may be a threat to powerful coalitions because it causes regroupings (for example, into new business units) which either add more value or are more central to the organization's success. The demise of the central planning units in the 1980s and the reduction of other centralized functions in the 1990s are such examples.

Groups may also feel their power is diminished if they begin to suffer from resource cutbacks, as their area is no longer regarded as critical to the organization. They watch amazed as resources are 'scandalously' poured into risky projects or new markets without an obvious and immediate payoff while they have had to justify every penny under the old regime. They may also feel resentful of the sunk costs which they invested in their jobs (for example, the time and energy that went into promoting certain products or services). Moreover, having to write off a misguided investment in a new product just before a change was introduced leaves the group open to attack through lack of vision and foresight.

These examples serve to illustrate the sensitivity and skills needed by those leading the change. However, spotting the potential troublemakers may be easier than actually doing something about them. Sometimes the problem will go away as the sources of power on which these individuals or groups were operating simply disappears (for example, the 'position power' of level in the hierarchy may no longer exist, the job may be less critical or the role of the expert becomes redundant). It may also be that, as the recognition and reward structure shifts away from dependence on the individual's appraisal by manager alone to 360-degree feedback, or the pay shifts from individual to group and organization bonuses, the 'reward power' of senior individuals declines. Other ways of overcoming this resistance is to use one's own 'network power' to counteract the propaganda put out by the resistors. Finally, these people may be transferred to a role in the middle of a critical mass of those who are for the change. They then have their negative influence swamped, so that they either have to change or leave.

8.10 INFLUENCING THE CULTURE

A general model of culture was put forward in Chapter 4 and explored with reference to quality. Therefore to change or sustain the quality culture, attention must be paid to the expression of the values, attitudes and norms within an organization in relation to its mission (Chapter 4, 4.3).

However, there are specific things which can be done to influence the culture, especially by the CEO. First, the CEO can influence what may be called destructive diversity. In many companies, there are particular functions which appear to dominate. For example, in General Electric, marketing is very influential. Promotions may come from within particular functions or stables and be dependent on education, background, or interests (e.g. golf and sailing). These cliques will often, by their nature, undermine a corporate culture since by definition they exclude others from the rewards which go with membership. A sensitive CEO will realize this and find ways to make the outcomes of candidate and promotion less of a foregone conclusion.

Destructive diversity may also be evident in parochialism, so that the amount of loyalty shown to a particular unit or group diverts attention from the corporate needs. A solution here is to move people laterally before they become too entrenched. Another way of coping with competition which becomes too negative is to control it with reference to an absolute standard (for example, the best at customer retention) rather than in a 'zero sum' game where one's gain is only at the expense of another's loss (as in battles over resources).

The second main area that can be influenced is the distance of the CEO from the grass roots. In some organizations, if the CEO wishes to exert control by merely checking a few key indicators, the stress on formal communications means that he or she has no intimate knowledge of what is going on. On the other hand, the CEO can encourage upward presentations so that the more junior managers can put forward ideas and, through their seniors' reactions, start to understand their values. While this can be risky because of the visibility, it does enable managers to see the values and behaviour relating to quality at a senior level. Encouragement of the questioning of policy can also be useful, related as it is to continual improvement. This means not just negative criticism; each presenter would have to add value with his or her comments. A hearing would therefore encourage middle management not to 'shoot the bearers of bad news' when they come with their problems, since it runs counter to the quality culture.

Thirdly, the CEO can influence the culture according to the way in which resources are allocated. Budgets and other resources enhance the status of a department. For example, if those related to boosting customer care are never refused funds (provided they make a business case) this will show the importance of this aspect of quality to the rest of the organization. Reductions in headcount at the centre also give the same message. Funds directed to improvement and innovation show that there is consistency between calls for innovation and reward for taking calculated risks. All these things signal what is valued.

Fourthly, the CEO can encourage people to challenge the traditional ways without appearing threatening or disloyal. There is a balance to be struck between an organization's need for some stability as a basis for efficiency and the need for change as a catalyst for learning and growth. Clearly, continual change results in organizational fatigue, even though gurus try to encourage people to 'love it'.

Finally, the CEO can endorse administrative practices or aid their decline. Whatever line is taken, it will indicate values. Take timesheets for example (common in project management or consultancy-based firms, sometimes recording in hours or quarter-of-an-hour units). Contrary to popular belief, the system cannot be easily manipulated. If utilization is higher than estimated against a project, this leads to loss of margin; if it is lower, it points to poor management of the individual or skills which are superfluous to requirements. Either way, it emphasizes short-termism, no state-of-the-art thinking or much training as there is no immediate payoff. The point is that managers will not do these things because they take time and that is constantly being costed. Developing products or personnel is thus neglected in favour of survival or crisis handling.

British Petroleum, for example,[2] underwent its culture change programme after the CEO began a series of workshops for senior managers, cascading it down the organization. The mnemonic used to encapsulate the required new behaviours was 'OPEN':

- *Open thinking* (not going for the first option; being open to the ideas of others);
- *Personal impact* (concern for impact, confidence, action);
- *Empowering* (team building, coaching, motivating);
- *Networking* (crossing boundaries to get the job done).

However, it will be noted that although the previous section related to CEO behaviour the model can be copied at any level of the organization.

8.11 IMPLEMENTATION DILEMMAS

Once it has been agreed that a particular approach or programme needs to be 'rolled out', there still remain a number of dilemmas which no package or particular consultancy approach can resolve. The decisions can only be made by those with detailed knowledge of the organization and its culture, with perhaps some advice on the implications and an eye to what has worked or not worked in other organizations. Leaders need to make judgements about what will work in their organization.

'Hard' versus 'soft' emphasis

First, there is the decision whether to emphasize the 'hard' aspects of the programme (such as costs, savings, customer-related improvements, the development of work methods), or the 'softer' side such as customer awareness and orientation, participative culture, mutual problem solving and learning from mistakes). Typically, the first group of behaviours may be successful in environments which are used to a high degree of structure and need some early, tangible results. However, the word 'emphasize' (not 'exclude') is used here advisedly. Without the softer side, the approach to quality improvement will not be sustained nor properly understood. For example, tighter process control and elimination of errors will be something that others have done to them rather than become a way of working that people do for themselves.

Big bang versus softly softly

Another problem is whether to have all the issues associated with the programme almost sorted out before going 'public' in the organization (for fear of generating uncertainty or raising expectations) or to say 'We have a decision in principle, we have mapped out where the problems are, but we must learn as we go'. Again, this might depend on the size of the organization, its previous experience with corporate changes and the homogeneity of the work done by the employees. In smaller units, 'learn as we go' may be less of a risk with good project management to react to and retrieve situations. By contrast, an organization with 100 000 staff may feel more comfortable with a more mechanistic and slower roll-out. This is because it is 'a big tanker to turn', and the consequences of faltering or poor logistics may reduce the ultimate commitment to change. If a very large critical mass is left disappointed with what has been done, it requires a lot of effort to neutralize attitudes before renewed attempts can be made.

Whole versus part

Should the whole of the organization go for the quality initiative or should certain parts be tackled first? Again, this may be heavily influenced by size. The part method (usually deliberately chosen for its chances of a high success rate or criticality to the core purpose of the organization) is useful to spearhead change, as those involved become ambassadors for the next 'wave'. These people have learned from their mistakes in a forgiving environment, since they are the pioneers and are expected to have overcome the teething troubles. A steady build-up of activities such as workshops, projects and communications is more likely to develop critical mass than 'stop-go' policies and sudden returns to the 'real job'. It is noteworthy here that for quality accreditation, awarding bodies allow sub-units (within a certain size range) to make applications separately from the larger parent organization.

Top down or bottom up

This question is always raised in change programmes. Top down refers only to the place at which to start training, not the imposition of philosophies and practices which are handed down as immutable. Bottom-up methods work only to the extent that resources and channels have been allocated to ensure that communications from this direction are heard, understood and actioned. The disadvantage is that there cannot be a wider perspective and accurate comparison of what is going on in other units.

Broad range versus single issue

In general, most of what has been said here refers to dilemmas before the project gets off the ground, but there are also issues to be resolved during the launch. For example, enthusiasm to tackle many things at once may outstrip capability. Does the organization prefer a panorama to tunnel vision? A broad range of quality-related issues may start to be tackled simultaneously: customer satisfaction, new technology and forms of measurement not used before. While there is a clear logic to all this, it may simply be too much for the organization to handle at once, and be introduced without any controls to see what is actually working well or making a difference. The other extreme produces an over-focusing on, for example, removal of defects or customer retention without considering the wider context that made these areas problematical in the first place.

Sledgehammer or scalpel

A related question is to do with the quality tools and techniques used to spearhead a programme. Sledgehammer or scalpel is the dilemma here. Sometimes the simple, precise and carefully applied tool will yield the most effective results. For example, one view[3] is that we have the tendency to ignore the simple techniques in our haste to use what are perceived to be the more complex, fashionable and high-power techniques and use them in isolation. Over-use of any tool, uncritically applied, can be harmful, not only because of the expectations that it will solve the problems but also that it stops the development of any further creative thinking.

Transition curves versus quantum leaps

Continuous or discontinuous change is another problem with which leaders have to wrestle. In any change, there comes a point where people have to be weaned off the old system. Classic cases are the customer record files which may be run in parallel until the new systems are working in a fail-safe manner. In one organization designing printed circuit boards, the management let the designers decide at what point the change-over to the new computer system would take place. On and after that date they were not allowed to use the old tools. There was no transition here; otherwise, it was felt, the motivation to get to grips with the new system would be lost.

Converts and deviants

Once the initial implementation is underway, it will be apparent who are the converts and who are the deviants. The dilemma is whether to transport the deviants into an environment where, by force of numbers, they have to give in, or to encourage their exit. A longer-term solution would be to change recruitment patterns so that only those comfortable with the new system were considered for selection. That is what BP did with its 'open' behaviours.

Message indifference or novelty fatigue

Finally, there is the dilemma of message indifference or novelty fatigue. Clearly, change needs to be fuelled and sustained by a consistent thread so that actions can be related back meaningfully to the overall thrust of the programme. However, after a while there is a danger that indifference may set in on what was once exciting and cause people to look elsewhere for stimulation. This leads people to refocus and rename their initiatives. At the other extreme (and probably related to the panorama versus tunnel vision and sledgehammer versus scalpel dilemmas), the organization uses too much change to keep up interest so that one change is never completed before another starts. In the end, novelty fatigue sets in.

8.12 CONCLUSION

This chapter has focused not on recipes for change in a textbook way (and there are many of these) but on attitudes, behaviours and problems with which leaders at different organizational levels will have to wrestle. The roles may be uncomfortable (being a change agent, influencing the culture if one is not a salesperson and working within the power structure if one is not a negotiator). The decisions may be difficult (contracting and managing external consultants or pondering the dilemmas). Retaining emotional objectivity may be a struggle (identifying key people, recognizing inhibitors of change and knowing when help is needed). However, leaders will have to display resilience in all these areas if they are to ensure that the changes they have to implement are successful.

ACTION QUESTIONS

- What steps does your organization take in preparing their managers (emotionally, behaviourally and in terms of skills) for the role of a change agent?
- What are the sources of power within your organization and where are they located?
- How can they be harnessed or neutralized in the service of quality management?
- Think back to previous changes you have known. What were the implementation dilemmas and how were they handled? Should they have been tackled differently?

REFERENCES

1 Wilson, D.C. (1992): *A Strategy for Change*, Routledge, London, UK.

2 Harrison, J. (1993): 'BP's Culture Change Programme', *Training and Development*, December, pp. 16-9.

3 Lascelles, D. and Dale, B.G. (1992): in Hand, M. and Plowman, B., *The Quality Management Handbook*, CIMA, UK.

CHAPTER 9

Management concerns and challenges

9.1 INTRODUCTION

While the overall concept of continuous improvement to deliver quality is accepted as vital to the success of any enterprise, there are nevertheless concerns surrounding the way in which this can be achieved and the challenges which its delivery imposes. Leaders have to confront them in a positive and creative way, as there are no 'textbook' answers. This chapter sets out to examine and explore them.

9.2 FAD OR FUNDAMENTAL FOUNDATION?

A common criticism now heard is that quality management (the word 'total' is often dropped) is yet another management fad likely to be overtaken by other approaches which will themselves be replaced. Its success as an idea has rested on an implicit assumption that in a changing world, it can offer the security of competitive advantage by the use of tools, techniques, and processes which enable the organization to be in control of itself (hence 'total'). Paradoxically, it can only achieve this security by continuous improvement and changing the status quo. An alternative view is that competition will itself be destructive and that new forms of cooperation will be the order of the day if countries and organizations are not to self-destruct. However, since partnerships or alliances will still depend on equitable exchanges, a product or service which is considered as worth bartering or incorporating into an organization will still need to be seen as one exhibiting quality; otherwise why should anyone be interested?

The broad reasons for failure of quality initiatives were outlined in

Chapter 1, 1.3 and will not be repeated here. However, there are some recurrent themes which seem to reinforce the label of 'fad' where quality management is concerned. Clearly, fads exist because of an organizational desire for a 'quick fix'. This is usually a reflex reaction of an organization in trouble or wanting something on a 'me too' basis.

The first classic manifestations in quality management are the sudden and rapid appearance of a number of activities, usually introduced without a quality strategy, in isolation and with over-ambitious expectations:

- *quality circles* (without organizational goals or context for quality);
- *customer care programmes* (without the supporting structures, resources and information);
- *empowerment* (responsibility but no authority and support);
- *BS5750* (without any value or understanding placed on the culture needed).

This kind of approach is usually doomed from the start, and leaves the senior management and everyone else reluctant to pursue the matter further.

The second major theme which perpetuates the notion of a fad is the reliance of quality management on tools and techniques as a substitute for thought. Cut adrift from the stabilizing influence and philosophical underpinnings, the tools may be used indiscriminately or without an appropriate managerial style. For example, with statistical process control, recording of errors may seem to be a 'hard' technique designed to bring to the surface the real problems. The difficulty is that if people find the results threatening, the data and resulting information will be protected to preserve the status quo and show that things are not so bad. Who wants to own a problem in a 'blame' culture?

Another sign of the 'fad' syndrome is that of the certainty which they purport to offer. Crosby's absolutes, Deming's imperatives and Juran's lists appear on paper to be logical and obvious lines to follow. Do all these things and success will surely follow is the message. Although their originators would probably never have intended it, they seem at first sight to offer a substitute for real analysis and careful application. The organization wants to 'plug them in' to solve its problems.

Fads, of themselves, cannot be blamed for lack of success. Any message suffers a loss of accuracy and sharpness in the course of repetition. Many of the philosophies, tools and techniques were personally implemented by their founders. As word spreads, disciples are recruited and the original ideas repackaged. As more people wish to buy the consultancy (or parts of it) the caveats become ignored until what often remains is a simplistic solution. These are all traps for the inexperienced or unwary purchasers and implementors alike. However, they are not insurmountable, and customers need to carefully re-examine their own motives before commitment (see Chapter 8, 4.8 Consultants).

9.3 CONTINUOUS IMPROVEMENT OR JUST GREAT EXPECTATIONS?

Continuous improvement (CI) is, to some, a philosophy which seems impossible when a product or service is acknowledged as being a leader in the field. Yet continuous improvement is the bedrock on which quality-oriented companies depend. While technology may play a large part in assisting this process, the mental attitude within the organization is critical. Four aspects have been identified[1].

First, there is 'escaping the tyranny of the served market'. This involves the company seeing itself as a portfolio of core competences rather than a portfolio of products. The example cited is that of Motorola viewing itself as a leader in wireless communications rather than as a producer of pagers and mobile 'phones. This permits it to explore various markets, such as local area computer networks.

Secondly, there is a searching for innovative product concepts which traditional market analyses are unlikely to uncover (for example, adding a new function to a well-known product (such as Yamaha's digital recording piano) or devising a new form of delivering a well-known function (automated tellers for dispensing money) or delivering a new functionality via a new product concept (for example, camcorders)).

Thirdly, there is the overturning of traditional price/performance assumptions that something first considered too costly can be marketed at an affordable price.

Finally, there is the ability to make the organizational presence felt in front of customers. Merely listening to what customers want is not enough. For example, how many customers would have wanted microwaves or CD-ROM computers? The same authors say that there are two kinds of companies regarding innovation: those who ask customers what they want and become followers; and those who lead customers where they want to go before they know it themselves. For example, NEC envisions a telephone which can interpret between callers speaking different languages.

The value of continuous improvement has been seen in Toyota Corporation. Seeking faster ways to develop low-quality cars, it became the benchmark in the automobile industry, reducing its new product development time to under two years. However, according to one source[2] its attempts at mass customization (tailoring products or services to a wider market) foundered because of the assumption that it was another step along the continuous improvement road. The authors argue that continuous improvement yields low-cost, high-quality standard goods and services, but that mass customization offers the same, except that it provides customized versions. The reasons they cite lie in the different organizational structures, values and managerial roles. In CI, teams bridge separate functions which interact in a predictable, sequential way, and operators do not question the essential design. Managers ensure that the links between the processes are tight and know how their function affects and is affected by others. They adopt a coaching role and encourage values which create a sense of community in the service of the organization and the customer.

Mass customization by contrast, it is argued, requires a dynamic network of relatively autonomous operating units which may not always combine in the same sequence or configuration. This is because the service provided is always changing in response to customer needs. The employees, too, are in a continuous learning mode. The manager's role here is in ensuring that the links between tasks or processes are in place to satisfy the many and varied customer requests. A key value is that placed on the diversity of employees' capabilities to meet the unpredictability of customer demands.

According to this thesis, Toyota's recent problems were that it had retained the organization structures and systems of continuous improvement while trying to pursue a mass customization philosophy. Instead of encouraging flexibility through a loose network, it tried to use its machines, such as robots, to reduce unwanted variability. The problem really lies in assessing which markets are appropriate for mass customization. For some markets, a large variety of offerings is inappropriate or unwanted. Continuous improvement will be viable only where markets are relatively stable and predictable. Where markets are highly turbulent because of changing customer needs or diminishing product life cycles, they are ready for customization. This distinction is not so sharp in practice, since many of the companies cited as representing the new mass customization (such as Motorola and Hewlett Packard) have traditionally been held up as CI quality companies and therefore cannot have done too badly by taking this route.

9.4 COMMITMENT TO QUALITY OR COMMITMENT TO AWARDS AND STANDARDS?

Talking to organizations who want to raise their standard of quality, there is usually a dilemma between trying to improve things internally for the customer and acquiring some form of external recognition for it. The latter path will involve them in extra time and cost, but they will acquire an added respectability in the eyes of their customers and the outside world in general. Once armed with these 'quality shields' they, in turn, will gain extra credibility and leverage when expecting higher quality from their own suppliers. The process and benefits of obtaining certain awards were dealt with in Chapter 6, and are therefore not the main focus of the discussion here.

If there is general agreement to apply for an award, there are a number of caveats, some general and some specific, to the award itself. For example, BS5750 is the standard which defines an organization's capability to consistently produce a product or service in a cost-effective and efficient way. It lays down a series of requirements which must be met in order for a company to become registered. The main thrust of the arguments against BS5750 are that, since it is more concerned with the presence or absence of systems, it does not ensure that quality is achieved. The process of registration and its maintenance, some argue, preoccupy the organization with a commitment to obtaining the standard rather than to improving the quality of the offering. This comes about through several ways:

- inundation with jargon
- over-emphasis on form filling
- too many complications in the standard
- over-reliance on consultants to help prepare the documentation for submission
- too many audits (diverting attention from the main tasks and preventing real improvements from being made as they will not be finished before the next audit)

- additional expense of consultants and audit fees
- excessive documentation in the required procedure manuals
- extra costs of recommendations if the standards are not met
- resolving problems of interpretation
- overcoming difficulties of fitting it into their business.

Yet such is the perceived pressure from customers, government bodies and fellow suppliers that well over 20 000 organizations have obtained the standard, and the trend is still upwards. The British Standards Institute, the prime accreditation body for BS5750, receives more than 5000 applications per year.

The dilemma seems to hit hardest with the small businesses who want to supply the larger ones which may insist on accreditation. One small business[3] with a sales turnover of under £1 million, paid £2,500 for consultancy in detailing areas of responsibility. Workshops for employees to learn new techniques cost £800, £250 was spent on the application, then there was an assessment charge of £1,750 and a further £520 to the certifying body. The company next had to hire extra staff costing £7,500 per annum and had to increase its prices by 14 per cent, losing 35 customers in the process.

The value of the auditing procedures to cover the 20 elements for assessment is that it makes people give answers to the following questions and then document them:

- How do you ensure that all operators of a procedure are trained?
- What internal audits are carried out?
- What processes are in place to review and improve the procedures?
- What statistical evidence exists to support these changes?
- How does the organization ensure that purchased products and services used in the procedures meet the standard?

This process will itself highlight inconsistencies and stimulate the organization to eliminate them. A classic slogan in the folklore of assessment says: 'Arguing with a QA auditor is like wrestling with a pig in mud: after a while, you realize the pig enjoys it'.

The point here is that any kind of assessment seems tough, but the process itself is valuable to the organization, even though it may feel uncomfortable.

The tendency in all this is to think of commitment to quality as compliance and standardization rather than as a focus on the customer.

Usually, as someone is responsible for meeting the standard, quality is seen as their job rather than that of all the staff. With TQM, the purpose is not merely to improve the systems but to transform the organization and its managers in the process of pursuing customer satisfaction and continuous improvement. Thus BS5750 is considered a building block for quality management, not a substitute for it. A commitment to standards and awards is not incompatible with the quality movement; the amount and variety of quality awards is a sign that, simply by taking part, organizations are making a statement about what they consider important. They show that the sponsors, givers and receivers of these awards are the leaders in the field. After all, prestigious organizations would not apply if they felt that it did not enhance their already well-known reputations for quality.

9.5 INTEGRATION OR DIVERSIFICATION?

The major quality awards were reviewed in Chapter 6. However, applying for any standard or quality award poses a challenge for an organization, both in terms of which to choose and allocating time, resources and money. For example, with the Malcolm Baldridge Award in the USA, companies apply by submitting a written application describing their quality management systems. These written applications (no more than 75 pages) have to provide answers to nearly 90 areas addressed for seven major categories. The evaluation begins with independent scoring of each submission by up to eight examiners.

Next, a panel of judges selects companies which are to continue to the next stage of the evaluation process. Those who do not pass receive a feedback report. For those continuing in the evaluation process, the examiners for an application reach a consensus in the scoring. A senior examiner's report is then produced and a site visit made by seven examiners who spend four days at a location. To conduct such a visit requires extensive advanced planning, after which judges then select the winners. A similar process operates for the European Quality Award and the UK Award, which are also based on self-assessment and site visits. The point is that the preparation generates alignment and cohesion in the organization, as the hosts do not know exactly who the examiners will visit or where they will focus their attention.

This and similar schemes beg the question for senior managers: Which one is the best for my organization? If I achieve this one rather than that one, what will be gained or lost in the process? The answer probably lies more with the purpose and sectors within which an enterprise operates than with the particular scheme in question. The initial process of self-assessment will yield insights into which framework is best suited and for whom.

There are obviously overlaps and similarities in all these awards. For example, customer satisfaction and leadership are in both the EFQM and Malcolm Baldridge schemes. The 'impact on the community' criterion of EFQM could also be taken to include concern with environmental standards, and BS5750 could be subsumed within the EFQM model's 'processes' criterion. Indeed, the recently instituted British Quality Award was conceived in consultation with the EFQM. The fact is that whichever framework is adopted it will help to clarify an organization's quest for quality.

9.6 BUSINESS PROCESS DESIGN: RE-ENGINEERING OR STRAITJACKET?

Business process re-engineering (BPR) is a topic which has gained favour as a new tool. Some see it as a replacement for total quality management: something to introduce some firmness into the culture-driven programmes; an alternative to the evolutionary, continuous improvement philosophy through the radical redesign of systems and procedures. There are many variants in the definitions of BPR. First, they usually contain elements such as 'fundamental rethinking', 'radical redesign', invention of new ways of working relating to business processes. Second, the aim is to improve operational performance in areas critical to the organization. Third, is the elimination of activities which do not add value to the customer or are not central to the process goals. Fourth, is the question of which processes to alter. Practitioners talk in terms of core processes, but which are they and at what level of detail does one operate? Some organizations choose activities related to critical success factors; others to the activities surrounding business or product streams; yet others home in on customer segments. Whatever the focus, the key question is how does it relate to the organization's strategic intent? Typical processes might be billing, supply chain management and new product development. Organizations generally use three criteria:

- *dysfunction* (which processes are in deepest trouble?)
- *importance* (which have most impact on the customer?)
- *feasibility* (which processes are most easily redesigned?).

For example, Rank Xerox identified nine key business processes, one of which was the customer order life cycle which received a high priority.

The process approach is designed to cut across the 'functional silos' and territoriality which often flourish in organizations for historical reasons. These groupings then maximize and defend their patch at the expense of the total business. The BPR process can be project-managed to deliver the required results in a speedy and timely fashion. Process re-engineering is not about using technology to support existing systems, but about rethinking the process design and the jobs that are needed to deliver it. Information technology has provided a powerful tool here in the sophistication of modelling it allows. It also has the ability to identify 'knock-on effects' (if the variables are altered) through the process if stages or resources are eliminated at different points. The aims and objectives of BPR are essentially: higher levels of customer service; greater productivity; and better overall quality of output. The four main steps are:

- *mobilization* (develop commitment; create a process map and select key areas; appoint process owners);
- *diagnosis* (select and scope the process and understand customer needs; understand the current process and identify weaknesses in the system; set targets for the new design);
- *redesign* (create breakthrough design concept; develop detailed process design and apply to business system; build prototype pilot and evaluate);
- *realization* (formulate implementation strategy; implement prototyping; develop supporting infrastructure and roll-out).

In fact, these general stages are no different from those of any change process.

Its greatest impact so far has been in the financial services sector, with productivity claims of between 40 and 60 per cent. For example, building societies handling mortgage applications have a workflow of processing the form, credit scoring and so on. With a model, one can build up a script of all the things which need to happen, when and in what sequence, so that a computerized system can track the item through against target times. Typically in the past, many items were delayed in the system waiting for signatures or conformity to legal requirements. Re-engineering the process can minimize the disruptive effects of this on the workflow and on the resources surrounding it. The effect of seasonal variation or peak transactions can be modelled in the system to see if it will cope. In terms of work measurement, it can eliminate much tedious work in conforming to legislative and accounting requirements through its ability to provide audit trails, work-in-progress and activity logs. In terms of managing the work, it enables the efficient handling of queries and work allocation, indicating whether or not targets are met, and may also assist in the diagnosis of problems, removing all activities not directly related to process goals. Companies who have chosen to use this tool include Ford, Philips, Kodak, British Airways, Texas Instruments, Midland Bank, Bank of England and Scottish Amicable. Ordnance Survey has used it for updating digital maps and Britannia Building Society for reorganizing arrears information.

Critics of the methodology will say that BPR is merely upmarket method study and operations research, enhanced by the capabilities of modern computing technology and the lessons learned from total quality management about mission, values, leadership and cross-functional teams. They point to the demise of Mutual Benefit Life, where the original pioneering work was done in the USA. The common criticisms are:

- Processes selected depend on the good judgement of senior management, otherwise they are too low-level to have much effect.
- No-one re-engineers his or her entire business and costs are prohibitive.
- If IT leads, poor structures may be transferred into state-of-the-art computerized, inefficient ones.
- You cannot talk about the processes without the people.
- Why should every process need discontinuous, radical change?
- It is the greenfield sites which are re-engineered, not the existing organization.
- It deskills jobs and is seen as another cost-cutting exercise.

A recent survey of 600 companies is quoted[4] as indicating that more than two-thirds of North American companies and three-quarters of European firms are re-engineering but that most have not seen a dramatic improvement in their business operations. Of those who reported poor results, 70 per cent said that ineffective project management was the cause and only 20 per cent had the backing of senior executives. The reason most commonly cited by 75 per cent of North American and 80 per cent of

European firms for introducing BPR was to cut costs. Revenue growth was rarely seen as a reason for using it.

While people delight in criticizing, there are some overlaps with TQM. First, BPR is strong on measurement and control and can incorporate quality targets along the way, giving management some immediate feedback on which to act. Secondly, since its origins lie in IT and quality, there is a focus on mission and vision, senior management commitment, customer focus and the need for careful change management. Thirdly, the quality management movement recognizes two kinds of improvement: *kaisen* (continuous) and *keiryo* (breakthrough). Successful organizations committed to quality have invariably combined both: the radical solution gives the stepwise leap which competitors soon copy. The differentiation is then based on the incremental improvements which push it to the limits until the time is right for the next discontinuous change.

9.7 IT: STEPPING STONE OR STUMBLING BLOCK?

Information technology has now become a fundamental part of the design, organization, support and delivery of services to customers. Emerging now are a number of issues which could affect the final offering.

In terms of influencing the company's image of quality, one of the most annoying problems is that of databases which become contaminated with inaccuracies. Even simple things like multiple mailings may be an irritation. Worse still, if insurance companies incorrectly enter one's address, higher premiums will be charged. As with computer fraud, companies are reluctant to admit they have any problems at all for fear of loss of image, the scrutiny of the Data Protection Registrar or angry customers.

With the ever growing requirement for more tailored services, it is important that organizations have reliable ways of capturing customer information and making it available to customer-facing staff. Integrated customer management information (or the function in which information about the customer is combined as necessary with information about the business) is seen as the way forward. For example, this approach has been used by Racing Green, the direct clothes retailer[5]. It chose a mail order package from the United States, and modified it to provide integrated operational and customer support. As this covers stock entry, management reporting and marketing, it allows the telephone operators (who cover seven days a week) quick access to information on the history of customer orders and stock availability.

Electronic data exchange of information is another way of improving the quality of products and services. The chemical company DuPont[6] found that it was using EDI and TQM techniques in isolation in its manufacturing processes. Data on suppliers and customers were being fed separately into its manufacturing computer systems to analyse specific product or process problems. A task force was set up and a pilot run carried out to integrate the two processes. Another application is that of brokers in the insurance industry, who could lose business if they do not adopt E-Mail when communicating with insurance companies, of whom more than 70 per cent are able to exchange information with them. This eliminates the lengthy process of printing or handwriting information which may later be transferred by phone or fax. Brokers are thus able to send requests simultaneously to a number of insurers who can reply instantly.

Poor information systems can lead organizations into difficulties with regulatory bodies. For example, Thames Water had sent out incorrect bills and reminders to customers while its information systems were being overhauled. OFWAT (the water industry regulatory body) has the power to cap the charges if it is dissatisfied with the service offered to customers.

There are also issues surrounding how customer systems operate. There is an increasing tendency in the UK towards offshore computing in third world countries. The finance sector is making the greatest use of these services (for example, Sun Life and Britannia Building Society). The two main uses are keyboard entry and transcribing large quantities of records and databases to new media such as CD-ROM. The simple reason is that, for example, in India, the cost of graduate programmers is ten times cheaper than in the UK and they are trained in languages which are in particular demand. Further competition comes from Eastern European countries and China who are now entering the labour market. As always, there are questions relating to quality not so much in terms of direct technical skills but in the project management of these areas. Secondly, there could be potential security problems – contract labour for hire in these situations may work for several organizations simultaneously, showing little real commitment or long-term loyalty to any of them.

Companies are now beginning to target their markets very carefully to acquire a market niche. To do this involves building sophisticated databases. Some mail order companies in the USA, for example[7], may capture up to 1400 pieces of information about a household, such as home ownership, appliance ownership and purchasing history, and develop statistical predictors as to who is likely to respond to particular promotions or use credit terms. Nevertheless, the compilation of these databases needs careful handling as it may be seen as an invasion of privacy. The core issue is whether the customer believes that he or she has voluntarily offered such information to a company. People's direct purchasing may be linked to a wider point-of-sale system with other information, so that the customer feels a loss of control concerning how the information is being used. While there are sometimes ways for customers to opt out, these systems may, by injudicious use, turn a strength of customer service into a weakness of real customer dissatisfaction, thus destroying any quality image being built up. In both Europe and the USA, regulation is being sought concerning the collection, use and transfer of personal information.

9.8 EMPOWERMENT OR ANARCHY?

Empowerment as a concept was covered in Chapter 7. Jan Carlzon's definition[8] is that its purpose is to:

> free someone from rigorous control by instructions and orders to give them freedom to take responsibility for their ideas and actions, and to release hidden resources which would otherwise remain inaccessible.

The cynics would say that there is nothing new in the concept of giving responsibility to people for what they do and thus gaining their commitment. The more critical believe that it is a vehicle for delayering, getting people to do more for less and, worst of all, is a recipe for loss of control.

However, the counter-arguments state that it is not a road to anarchy, for several reasons. First, organizations still need to spell out for people the end results, the performance required and the competencies to achieve them. Secondly, individuals and groups are encouraged to measure their own performance, and their boundaries of responsibility are still defined. What is not formalized is the way in which empowered employees go about achieving these ends. Thirdly, in a quality-oriented organization, the very fact that there are internal customers for each role means that there are built-in checks and balances. Some companies, like Harvester and Frizzell Financial Services, now issue written guidelines where once they were oral and informal. Then there are the overall mission and values which serve as a guide to decisions and actions which may themselves be constrained by the information tools with which employees work. Last, but probably the most critical, enabling factor is the style of the immediate line manager (Chapter 4), which will determine how mistakes are handled, the learning that occurs and its transfer to the rest of the team.

At Frizzell, for example, the consumer advisers are expected[9] to be logged into the computer for 90 per cent of the time that they are in the office and on the phone for at least 50 per cent of the day. They can exceed targets, but if they fail to meet them the team manager will discuss why and what problems were encountered. In addition, each person has a statement of expectations, defining what the team manager will expect and vice versa. These cover areas ranging from courtesy and cheerfulness to 'never turn a blind eye to something you think is wrong or silly'. The importance of the right mental attitude here is echoed by CIBA-Geigy's head of management development who said that: 'Empower is not a verb; 'you' cannot empower 'me'. It is more a state of mind and way of working.'

9.9 MANAGING QUALITY IN NEW ORGANIZATIONAL FORMS: POSSIBILITY OR PIPE DREAM?

There is an increasing trend to outsourcing across all main industrial and commercial sectors and for many functions, especially IT (see earlier in this chapter). This raises the question of whether and how quality of service can be maintained. In some cases it is not a question of economy but enhancement. For example, Apple Computers awarded a multi-million-pound outsourcing contract to BT. This was for the running of its new 24 hour-a-day customer support operation Apple Assistance[10] to improve help offered in dealing with product-related problems. British Telecom will install and operate multilingual Apple customer support centres in the UK and in France and staff will be provided with extensive product information to meet certain performance targets.

Sedgwick, the insurance giant, has outsourced the management of its voice, data and messaging networks. It will cover all facilities, from telephones on the desks to the brokers' local area networks. The Sedgwick director[11] responsible was quoted as saying: 'We want expertise for the future, not the past', and found that for its private network 'it would be cheaper to upgrade it by outsourcing rather than through further capital outlay'. Quality would be further improved by internal staff being freed from day-to-day management to concentrate on the strategic uses of IT.

So much for the concept, but how can users with facilities management contracts ensure that they get the quality of service they want? While trust and good relations are important, contracts can go wrong. Three commonly reported problems[12] are:

- ownership and exploitation of software developed for users by the services suppliers
- user arrangements for terminating the contracts of the staff
- damages for failing to meet agreed service levels.

All these need to be carefully considered when the contract is drawn up.

A factor related to quality is the degree of control the user has over its resources and assets. Some organizations may wish to retain strategic control over hardware and software. If things are not successful, the contract can be terminated and the user still has the equipment and the budget, and the service can still be maintained. Sedgwick, while outsourcing most of its systems, still retains control of its global electronic network.

To maintain guarantees of quality of service, users need to specify performance measures based on the type of dimensions of quality they wish to offer. For example, Brighton Borough Council[13] obtains service credits from its outsourced IT supplier based on availability and response times. Others maintain that if the service drops even lower, penalty points are incurred and a refund is made. The idea is that, to retain control, the contract should be specified by the user and performance criteria for the service linked to the main or most important areas of the business.

Apart from IT outsourcing, there are instances of organizations spinning off subsidiaries to serve them as a priority customer while generating external revenue. For example, several consulting engineering firms have evolved recruitment agencies to service their own needs. These are given the names of ex-employees and it is thus easier to maintain quality in these circumstances, as staff are known to the company.

There are also a number of spin-off consultancies which organizations use when they need to obtain outside help. They are staffed, at least in part, by former employees who know the standards required. For example, IBM set up Skillbase, BA has Speedwing Technologies and Cable and Wireless has Coreskills. BA Technologies is a holding company for business developed from its information management function. It sells IT products and services on the open market. The insurance industry is also one which has used the flexibility of working arrangements to advantage. The self-employed associates of Allied Dunbar selling financial services undergo training tied to selling products. The right to progress to selling more complex or high return products requires a licence ensuring that the necessary training is not avoided by the associates. These steps are ways of building in quality assurance to the customer and avoiding the accusation of selling inappropriate goods.

With the changing structures of organizations, it is crucial to understand the possible effects on the delivery of a quality service. Clearly, clarity in performance and contractual services is a must, but there is also an issue about how far organizations offer training and development which is to mutual advantage. If professionals are treated as 'jobbing freelances' merely to aid numerical flexibility and economy, then commitment will fall, as will the quality. Allegiance will be given to several organizations and the strongest candidates will go to those who treat them as extensions of themselves rather than as convenient add-ons. That is when the idea of a flexible, quality-based organization will be more than a pipe dream.

9.10 QUALITY AND ENVIRONMENT: HOPE OR HYPE?

Managers often ask concerning total quality programmes 'Where next?' The environmental enthusiasts point in their direction. The arguments run something like this. Customer perceptions and loyalty are increasingly being shaped by an organization's performance. New environmental standards and regulations are having an effect on the running of the business in the same way as quality standards have done. Whether in an office or on the shop floor, good environmental policies are said to pay for themselves. The sort of topics referred to here cover: waste management and recycling; new materials impact on the environment; and design for health. Companies may find themselves increasingly in a round of attack and counter-attack on what they are doing, which has prompted a 'life cycle analysis' (LCA) approach in their defence. This involves examining the environmental effects of a product or service at every stage from raw material extraction and production to disposal. The purpose is to: substantiate claims made in green advertising; fend off unwarranted regulatory pressure; and reduce the polluting impact of products.

British Telecom is one of the businesses which sees a link between quality and environmental management as a way of developing a competitive advantage and improving customer and shareholder satisfaction. The company has a nine-point policy for minimizing the impact of its operations on the environment by means of a programme of continuous improvement. Only the first point will be quoted here, but the reader will pick up echoes of quality policies:

> meet, and where appropriate, exceed the requirements of all relevant legislation. Where no regulations exist BT will set its own exacting standards.

Its customers are asking similar questions about environmental policies. For example, a government department required, as part of the contract, that BT had the ability to undertake an environmental impact assessment of the project. Birmingham City Council, Shell UK, County NatWest, and the Great British Lottery Company are all organizations which have requested such information. British Telecom now offers an internal helpline if staff receive an environmental questionnaire from a customer and are not sure of the answers.

British Telecom is also overseeing the role of engineers, as they have a key role to play under environmental legislation which places a duty of care on the company and its staff to ensure that all unwanted, obsolete equipment is disposed of in a responsible manner. Scrap is then forwarded to recycling agencies who have themselves undergone a BT environmental audit and who only deal with 'quality disposal companies'. For example, less scrupulous scrap cable companies may burn off the sheathing in an open fire, thus polluting the atmosphere. With 12 000 tonnes of scrap cable per year, this could be a serious problem. As a result, BT has its own environmental audit manager with a dedicated team.

The environmental standard BS7750 was reissued in 1994 to accommodate revisions, for further and higher education. Critics fear, however, that the standard is putting off universities and that they will avoid developing environmental improvement policies (for example, a transport policy that discourages cars in favour of bicycles on campuses). However, it does not have to demonstrate that its environmental impact has improved, merely that processes have been put in place so that it could improve if necessary. This could mean a 3–5 year programme but those where BS5750 has already been installed would find it easier to implement.

As long ago as 1972[13] the idea was being proposed that the cost of poor quality was much more than errors and omissions in the production process. There was the cost of damage done by the new product to society and there were others:

- resource not available to the next generation
- disposal costs as a result of items wearing out or failing
- impact on society and the environment of the product while in use.

The prophetic nature of these statements can be traced respectively in the endangering of the tropical rainforests, disposal difficulties of plastics and nuclear waste, and traffic pollution.

It will be noticed that the last area (impact on society) is one of the key 'result' areas in the EFQM model. Royal Mail, for example, has increased its involvement in community projects as a result of its application of the model to its own self-assessment. Some environmental charities are offering training schemes in return for sponsorship. Boots, Ford and local authorities have all been involved. Senior Post Office managers have worked in the Czech Republic to examine the impact of acid rain on the forests of Bohemia. Using their skills in computing, accountancy, sales, marketing and management, they worked with scientists to produce a practical report for action. The advantage of the training received was that it was in real life, environmental projects and was to help them work as a team.

9.11 ORGANIZATIONAL ETHICS AND QUALITY: COMPLIANCE OR INTEGRITY?

By encouraging ethically conscious cultures and behaviours, managers can boost the relationship and reputations (and hence quality image) on which their companies depend, thus giving them a competitive edge. This is what the evidence from the United States seems to be saying. Traditionally, ethics has been thought of as a purely personal matter with transgressions being the result of a flawed character. Another view[14] maintains that ethics has everything to do with an organization and its management. The reason for this is that unethical business practice involves the tacit, if not the explicit, cooperation of others and reflects the values and culture of the organization. In fact, the same authority has gone so far as to state:

> Managers who fail to provide proper leadership and to institute systems that facilitate ethical conduct share the responsibility with those who conceive, execute and knowingly benefit from corporate misdeeds.

Those who ignore ethics risk personal and corporate liability. Secondly, it is said, they deprive organizations of the benefits of the federal guidelines for sentencing organizations. This recognizes the organizational and managerial basis for unlawful conduct. It also imposes fines partly on the preventive measures which companies have taken to discourage misconduct. As a result, many companies are quickly installing compliance-based ethics programmes to prevent, detect and punish legal violations. It is obvious that rule books and a culture of avoiding illegal practice is a very negative approach. Ethics based on integrity rather than on compliance is not a problem if organizations have mission and values statements, as 'quality'-oriented companies certainly do!

An interesting illustration of the situation is given by the same author. Clearly, if customer satisfaction or quality had been one of the corporate values, it is difficult to see how the situation would have arisen in the first place. Sears, Roebuck and Company, who run an automotive service business, were deluged with complaints from consumers in more than 40 states. The company stood accused of selling unnecessary parts and services. The problem was not just individual behaviour – Sears management tried to increase the financial performance of its centres by introducing goals and incentives which created a fertile climate for abuse. Service advisers were given product sales quotas and paid a commission. Failure to achieve these targets could result in transfer or a reduction in work hours. In fact, the omission of management to clarify the fine distinction between unnecessary service and legitimate preventive maintenance, along with consumer ignorance, fuelled the situation. The company denied that it deliberately tried to deceive consumers and withdrew its commission and quotas. It began a series of unannounced shopping audits and made plans to make its own internal monitoring more rigorous. Both of these measures are commonplace in quality-focused organizations. In fact, the settlement was around US$60 million, a huge sum for the cost of poor quality service.

A distinction has been drawn between compliance-based ethics and integrity-based ethics. Basically, the former is concerned with conformance to externally imposed standards, not self-governance with chosen ones. The objective is to prevent criminal misconduct rather than enable responsible conduct and is primarily lawyer-driven. The standards are those of the criminal and regulatory law rather than of company values and aspirations supported by the law. In fact, the same distinctions could apply to organizations following BS5750 as a preferred path rather than the total quality route. Some organizations have even set up ethics networks to encourage internal, anonymous enquiries and concerns of staff to be followed up. Their role here is to serve as an early warning system for poor management and safety defects.

9.12 CONCLUSION

The concerns and challenges that have been covered in this chapter are those without easy answers. The solutions that are found depend heavily on the context and culture of the organization. Nor are they knowledge-based or dependent on the simple application of tools and techniques. Experience, courage, and some fundamental thinking are the most reliable guides. If these matters can be satisfactorily resolved within the strategic framework of the organization, then there will have truly been leadership for quality.

ACTION QUESTIONS

- How is the value of continuous improvement translated into action in your organization?
- What indicators do you have to show how information management is affecting the quality of the service your organization delivers?
- Is your organization adopting new forms? If so, what action is being

taken to see that they are not affecting quality and are actually enhancing it?

REFERENCES

1 Hamel, G. and Prahalad (1991): 'Corporate Imagination and Expeditionary Marketing', *Harvard Business Review*, July/August, pp. 81–92.

2 Pine, B.J., Victor, B. and Boynton, A. (1993): 'Making Mass Customization Work', *Harvard Business Review*, September/October, pp. 108-19.

3 Bethell, J. (1993): 'Small Firms Head Revolt Against Quality Standard', *Sunday Times*, Small Business Focus, p. 12.

4 IPM (1994): 'Poor Planning Leads to High Failure Rate in Business Re-engineering', *Personnel Management*, August, p. 6.

5 Goodwin, C. (1993): 'When the Customer is King', *Computer Weekly*, 11 November, pp. 30-2.

6 Dudman, J. (1993): 'Better by Communication', *Computer Weekly*, 11 November, p. 34.

7 Bessen, J. (1993): 'Riding the Marketing Information Wave', *Harvard Business Review*, September/October, pp. 151-60.

8 Carlzon, J. (1987): *Moments of Truth*, Ballinger Publishing Company, Wisconsin, USA.

9 Pickard, J. (1993): 'The Real Meaning of Empowerment', *Personnel Management*, November, pp. 28-33.

10 Snell, T. (1994): 'Apple Outsource to BT as IBM Alliance Rumours Grow', *Computing*, 27 October, p. 11.

11 Ward, M. (1993): 'Mercury Wins £20M Facilities Management Deal', *Computer Weekly*, 15 July, p. 2.

12 Warren, I. (1994): 'Contract Killing', *Computer Weekly*, 18 August, p. 22.

13 Hodson, H.V. (1972): *The Diseconomies of Growth*, Earth Island, London, UK.

14 Paine, L.S. (1994): 'Managing for Organizational Integrity', *Harvard Business Review*, March/April, pp. 106-17.

Index